Broadway Books

NEW YORK

Daily Adventures
in a Parisian Kitchen

CLOTILDE DUSOULIER

PUBLISHED BY BROADWAY BOOKS

Copyright © 2007 by Clotilde Dusoulier

Published in the United States by Broadway Books,
an imprint of The Doubleday Broadway
Publishing Group, a division of
Random House, Inc., New York.
www.broadwaybooks.com

BROADWAY BOOKS and its logo, a letter B bisected on
the diagonal, are trademarks of Random House, Inc.

Library of Congress Cataloging-in-Publication Data

Dusoulier, Clotilde, 1979–
Chocolate & zucchini : daily adventures in a
Parisian kitchen / Clotilde Dusoulier. —1st ed.
p. cm.
Includes index.
1. Cookery, French. I. Title. II. Title: Chocolate
and zucchini.

TX719.D867 2007
641.5'944—dc22

ISBN-13: 978-0-7679-2383-5
ISBN-10: 0-7679-2383-9

PRINTED IN JAPAN

1 3 5 7 9 10 8 6 4 2

First Edition

For *Maxence*

Contents

ACKNOWLEDGMENTS

I would like to thank Maxence for his unfailing support, wisdom, and love. My parents and my sister, Céline, for laughing at my jokes. My mother and my grandmother, for providing the soil in which my cooking could grow. My neighbors Stephan and Patricia, for all the meals we've shared. My dearest friends — Alisa, Marie-Laure, Laurence, and Marion in particular — for cheering me on, and letting me test recipes on them.

I would also like to thank Lenn Thompson for creating the splendid wine pairings in this book. My agent and friend Claudia Cross, for her precious advice and her ever-smiling voice. The Broadway Books team — especially Jennifer Josephy, my editor, and Kristen Green, her assistant — for bringing the book to life.

Finally, I want to express my gratitude to the visitors of the *Chocolate & Zucchini* Web site, for reading what I have to say and coming back the next day — this book wouldn't exist if it weren't for you.

Special thanks to the *Chocolate & Zucchini* readers who cross-tested the recipes in this book: for their time and thoughtful notes, let me acknowledge Neil Aird, Elaine Anderson, Janice Barton, Teresa Bauer, Lisette Bonilla, Heather Brush, Melissa Capyk, Julie Conason, Maryanne Conroy-Miller, Cynthia Flock, Charity Hanif, Melissa Harp, Mary Sue Hayward, Vanessa Hodge, Shauna James, Julie Jendresky, Erin Jimcosky,

Glen Kanwit, Tatiana Kharitonova, Samantha Koss, Faith Kramer, Sharon Leger Gottula, Elizabeth MacCrellish, Alyce Mantia, Carrie McMahon, Adele Miller, Patricia Moore, Melissa Newman, Walter and April Nissen, Tara O'Brady, Marzi Pecen and Monkey, Kenneth Pocek, Ann Riley, Suzy Russinoff, Derrick and Melissa Schneider, Rainey Smith, Donna Smith-Harrison, Emelda Valadez, and Melinda Way.

Foreword

Food joyously occupies a large portion of my waking thoughts — it even makes appearances in my dreams — and I find pleasure in every single one of its facets: the shopping, the looking, the talking, the reading, the thinking, the chopping, the kneading, the sharing, and of course, the eating.

I love nothing more than trying a new restaurant, studying the menu carefully, and debating over which dish to choose. Happening upon an unusual vegetable, and finding a flattering use for it. Reading about a recipe, a chef, a technique, and jotting down the ideas that spark up. Lifting the lid from a pot of stew, cajoling dough into coming together in my hands, or watching through the oven door as my soufflés puff up. Daydreaming about menus, inventing dishes, and if I'm lucky, having them turn out better than I expected. Inviting friends over, calling them to the table as I bring forth a steaming dish, and seeing their expectant faces light up.

I find it hard to imagine now, but I wasn't always like this: as a child and a teenager, I didn't give much thought to food. My mother was — and still is — an excellent cook, and I liked to sit in the kitchen as she prepared our meals, or bake with her on lazy Sunday afternoons. But as soon as I got up from the family table, my mind turned to other matters.

There were things I knew I liked, things I thought I didn't, and I wasn't in the least adventurous. I loved the plastic-wrapped Gruyère from the grocery store and wouldn't touch the oozy Reblochon from the farm. Square slices of white bread were largely favored over the artisan loaves my parents enjoyed, and I kept the same breakfast routine for years on end. To me, eating was like breathing: something I did naturally, and without thinking. It was an enjoyable activity, but I took it for granted and didn't feel the need to celebrate it.

This all changed, practically overnight, when I moved with my boyfriend, Maxence, to the San Francisco Bay Area after our graduation: it was the height of the dot-com years and there was work aplenty for the software engineer.

I had always been drawn to the lifestyle and culture of America, as seen through a myriad of books and movies, and I was thrilled to experience them firsthand. Everything was cause for wonder and surprise, and I wrote endless e-mails to my family and friends in Paris, detailing my thoughts and discoveries as I settled into this new life.

But what made the sharpest impression on me was the food, and its sheer novelty: dishes and specialties I'd never heard of, gigantic grocery stores with entire aisles devoted to breakfast cereals, unknown ingredients, and muffins so big you needed both hands to hold them. Food, food everywhere, as far as the eye could see — I was fascinated.

Never before had I had to cook or buy food on a daily basis, and learning to do so in a foreign country was even more intense an experience. I was stepping into a whole new world, one I had never suspected was so rich, so multidimensional, and above all, such fun.

What better place than California to get interested in food, with its wealth of fresh produce, gourmet shops, and talented chefs? I spent hours exploring every food store in my path, buying cartloads of ingredients I barely knew what to do with, filling the house with books and cooking gear, calling my mother for advice, and experimenting in the kitchen.

I felt as if I had just awakened after years of gastronomic hibernation. I wanted to dine at every restaurant, try every ethnic cuisine, and learn all about the history and culture of food. Rummaging through my mind for buried food memories, I wanted to recapture those flavors, give a new chance to every ingredient I'd always wrinkled my nose at, challenge my cooking abilities, and see where this would take me.

Soon enough my tastes broadened, my palate sharpened, and it was finally revealed to me that stinky cheese on peasant bread was as close to bliss as one could possibly get.

⳥⳩⳥

When Maxence and I returned to France after two years in California, another food culture shock awaited me. With my freshly opened eyes, I reacquainted myself with the food dimension of life in Paris, a fundamental aspect I had never really experienced, but had nonetheless dimly missed in the States. And if the Bay Area was a fantastic playground for food enthusiasts, then Paris, with more bakeries per capita than one would think possible, appeared to me like heaven.

(At the same time, now that I was back on the other side of the mirror, I found myself developing a brand-new kind of nostalgia: I started yearning for chunky peanut butter, serious burgers, fluffy pancakes, and a particular kind of cinnamon puffed cereal.)

It was in Paris that I started cooking for my friends and family, something I seldom did in California, where our social occasions were more about dining out than dining in. I discovered the growing excitement, the joy of sharing food, and the blushing pride of putting together a meal that your friends relish and may still talk about for months afterward.

⳥⳩⳥

So I cooked, and shopped, and ate, and cooked again, and this made me very happy. But soon enough, I realized how ephemeral this all was: hours of thought and handiwork were consumed in a matter of minutes. Although this had a beauty of sorts, it was a little frustrating, and I found that the best way to make up for the fleeting nature of my passion was to write.

It started with a simple notebook, in which I wrote what I cooked, when and for whom, how it had turned out, and how it could be improved. It is around that time that I discovered food blogs, online cooking journals written by home cooks: I quickly became an avid reader of the handful that existed back then — this was 2003 — and a few months later, started my own.

I named it *Chocolate & Zucchini* to illustrate the two facets of my cooking personality: on the zucchini side is my love of vegetables, my preference for healthy and natural foods; and on the flip side of the coin is my decidedly marked taste for all things sweet, and chocolate, glorious chocolate, in particular.

The *Chocolate & Zucchini* Web site took shape day by day, as I shared my culinary adventures and gastronomic pursuits. Much to my surprise, the traffic steadily increased, and I got more and more messages from readers who felt a connection to me and found inspiration in my writing. This could not have pleased me more.

Maintaining a blog takes time, but the gratification went far beyond what I had imagined. Not only did I finally feel that I was building something, but it also revealed myself to myself: how passionate I was about food and writing, and how deeply I yearned for a career change. And as I started to explore the ways in which I could make a living out of this passion, the blog proved an invaluable source of opportunities. It allowed me to test-drive a variety of food-related activities, and gave me a chance to meet many of the chefs and writers whose work I had long admired.

Two years after launching *Chocolate & Zucchini*, after carefully listening to what I wanted deep inside and considering my options, I decided I was ready for that leap of faith. I quit my day job and started a new life as a full-time writer.

ABOUT THE BOOK

The idea of a book had been on my mind for some time. Over all these months of writing on my Web site, I had seen a tiny universe take shape: *Chocolate & Zucchini*, as a dining table to which one twenty-something Parisian invites the rest of the world, had taken on a life of its own, and I felt this was worth celebrating in book form.

As a passionate reader and book lover, I find that a book — the object itself, the weight in your hands, the presence on your bedside table — has a personality and charm that a Web site can never hope to achieve. It's hard to take a Web site in the kitchen with you, or curl up with it on the couch, a mug of tea by your side and the cat on your lap. You cannot scribble things in the margin of a Web site, or accidentally smudge a little batter on it, forever marking that recipe as the stupendous cake you made for your sister's birthday.

These are some of the reasons why I wrote the book you are now holding. I wanted to gather a book's worth of things I enjoy, things I've learned over time, things that make me happy — and share them with you.

ABOUT THE RECIPES

In this book you will find a collection of new creations and old favorites. Each recipe comes with a story, because we all know that a dish is much more than a list of ingredients and a set of instructions: it draws its life and color from its backdrop, its emotional setting, and the little anecdotes of its genesis.

My main focus is on fresh and seasonal ingredients, and the recipes are designed to let their flavors sing. The quality of the ingredients you choose will make or break them, and I can only encourage you to seek out the best you can find and afford. It will make all the difference in the world.

All recipes were tested at least three times by readers of *Chocolate & Zucchini*, and I have done my best to make them precise and easy to follow. But however exacting a recipe writer tries to be, the experience of each cook will vary depending on the specific ingredients and appliances that he uses or even the atmospheric conditions, and you should always trust your instincts and your senses over anything a recipe says.

ABOUT THE WINE PAIRINGS

My food and wine pairing skills are rather basic: once in a blue moon I know just what I need — I may have read about it, or tasted a similar pairing before and liked how it fared — but most of the time I simply walk to my favorite wine shop and ask my *caviste* for advice. I describe the dish; he hums for a few seconds (the longer the hum, the trickier the pairing) and points me to the recommended bottle, which may boast a pink heart-shaped sticker that reads *coup de coeur maison* if it's a particular showstopper.

If you have a wine store near you with a friendly staff that will provide the same service (with or without the heart-shaped stickers), add it to your running list of blessings. But if you don't, no worries: I have asked wine writer Lenn Thompson (of lenndevours.com) to create pairing suggestions for this book. You will find them below the recipes, with his tasting notes. If you're anything like me, they will make you want to run out for that bottle and uncork it with your bare teeth.

However, no pairing is ever set in stone: Lenn has focused on affordable and widely available wines, but there are plenty of alternatives for you to explore — smaller wineries, older vintages, or pricier bottles. Consider these suggestions as an example of what will work, and take it from there.

ABOUT THE PHOTOGRAPHY

The photography in this book is by yours truly. I have always felt that the pictures I take for my Web site play an important part in conveying my excitement about a dish — just as important as the story or the recipe itself — and I wanted to keep this personal touch. The photos were styled and shot in my apartment, in natural light, using dinnerware plucked from my own cabinets. No food was harmed in this process — no wood glue, no hairspray, no glycerin — and all dishes were happily consumed afterward, after a bit of reheating when necessary.

Ma Philosophie de Cuisine

MY COOKING PHILOSOPHY

*M*eeting fellow food enthusiasts is a bit like reconnecting with long-lost friends. It takes just a glance and a few words to recognize them, and soon enough a feeling of mutual understanding, of natural ease, sets in: you belong to the same club, speak the same language, and share the same values about life, and the enjoyment thereof.

I have found that there are many different shades to this passion, and I am most curious about other people's cooking philosophy: what draws them into the kitchen, and what do they find there? What makes them tick, what fascinates them, what keeps them awake at night, their stomach rumbling so loudly the neighbors might complain? And when in turn they ask to hear about mine, I find myself invoking the words "ingredients," "curiosity," "creativity," and "pleasure."

INGREDIENTS

Nothing provides me with such inspiration as finding a rare or quirky ingredient to experiment with, seeing the new season's bounty appear on market stalls and plucking my share gleefully, or talking to a food artisan and having him explain the finer points of his craft. Excitement, joy, respect — these are the feelings that pull me along into the kitchen to play.

Cooking is primarily about loving your ingredients and letting them shine through. It's about choosing them with care and at their peak, and using them in a way that appeals to your own tastes, but never betrays their personality, or muffles what they have to say. And if you treat your ingredients kindly, if you invite them into a dish with like-minded ingredients and judicious seasoning, they will repay your efforts on your plate, and on your palate.

CURIOSITY

I am a curious person at heart. This is true in all areas of life, but especially when it comes to food and cooking. I am constantly itching to find out and understand where ingredients come from, who produces them and how, where and when to buy them; why recipes work, what traditions they're rooted in, and what historical and cultural reasons are responsible for their creation. So I ask questions ("Too many," grumpy waiters might tell you), I look things up, and I try to learn as much as I can.

And the wonderful thing is, if you are curious about the characteristics and qualities of your food, if you explore the world, starting right at your doorstep, through food habits and culinary customs, you will be that much wiser. Not only will you derive more pleasure from your eating and your cooking, but this knowledge will also become second nature, guiding your hand to make the most of what's available.

Luckily, the galaxy of food knows no bounds: you could travel for the rest of your life, wander through every market, trade recipes with every person you meet, try every dish that you smell from every open window, and still entire worlds would remain, waiting for you to discover and taste your way through them. (Excuse me while I clap my hands in excitement.)

CREATIVITY

As a child, I loved fiddling with things, deconstructing toys and objects, and trying to get them back together afterward. Duct tape and scissors were my very good friends, and I liked to use my mother's sewing machine to assemble miniature purses and hair scrunchies with fabric from her big treasure chest of scraps. I wouldn't go so far as to call myself crafty, as nothing earth-shattering ever emerged from my hands, but I loved how these activities sucked me in, making me lose all sense of time until suddenly I looked up, night had fallen, and it was time for dinner.

As I grew older I gradually stopped doing these things, mostly for lack of time (and perhaps toys to disassemble), but it is clearly this side of my personality that led me to cooking. At a point in my life when my day job made me feel frustrated, expressing little and creating nothing of real worth, I found myself yearning for the kitchen as a place where I could do my own thing, play with colors, smells, and flavors, see the magic at work, and feed my friends.

And I have found that cooking creativity is a skill that can be cultivated: as you gain experience, your instincts take the driver's seat, and you don't really need to follow recipes too closely anymore.

Keeping a Food Journal

Whether in a notebook, on your computer, or as a food blog, it is helpful to keep a cooking journal: write down the name of the dish, what recipe you used and your modifications, which occasion and whom you made it for (the self-respecting host would rather die than accidentally serve a dish twice to the same guest, you see). Add your comments, however short or detailed you want to make them.

Jot down the interesting dishes that you taste at restaurants, the projects you want to take on, the unusual food pairings you hear about, and more generally, the random thoughts that pop into your mind. (Inspiration can strike at any time, in any place. Some of my best ideas came to me on the métro, at the opera, or during lengthy work meetings, so I make sure I take my pen and notebook wherever I go.)

You can refer to your notes when you're looking for inspiration, or when you want to elaborate on a dish you've cooked before. This will help you build on your experience, keep track of your progress, and watch the evolution of your culinary personality.

Organizing Your Cookbooks and Clippings

If you are like most enthusiastic cooks, your shelves are probably laden with an everexpanding collection of cookbooks, recipes copied from Web sites, and others clipped from magazines. How do you organize all this and capitalize on this wealth of ideas? In my world, the cookbooks get spiked with sticky flags that mark the appealing dishes, the online recipes are kept in a file on my computer, and the clippings are sorted in a cardboard folder. But organization is a personal thing, and you should devise the system that works for you. Whichever one you choose, the idea remains the same: to map out the scenery of your collection, and make it easy for you to find your way around.

While it's tempting to hoard a huge amount of recipes, it's best to keep or tag only the ones that really inspire you, the ones you think you'll get around to trying someday — no, *really*. And, of course, it's not much use to file recipes away if they never see the light of day. But if you go through your cookbooks and folders on a regular basis — when you're planning a dinner party or have to take a dish somewhere — their content will live someplace fresh in your mind, ready to be called upon when you see something unusual at the market: "Sea spinach? Aha! I have a recipe for this!"

Cooking from the Pantry

As a little exercise to flex your creative muscles, try this: open the fridge, look through your pantry, and improvise a dish — or better yet, an entire meal — using only what you have on hand. No shopping allowed. You can refer to existing recipes (that's when you'll be glad you've kept your cookbooks and clippings organized), but you will likely have to adapt them, and this is where it gets interesting.

This approach, focusing on available ingredients rather than a finished product, is the best way to let loose, unleash your own ideas, and make the most of your food supplies. If you've never really cooked like this before, it may seem a little daunting, like riding a bike without the training wheels. You may fall and scratch your knee every once in a while, but you will always learn something from it, and most of the time you will be surprised, and oh-so-proud, to see how well you do on your own. (Don't forget to write down the recipe then.)

PLEASURE

Ultimately, the most valuable thing to be found in cooking is pleasure. Pleasure of the five senses — the lush colors of fresh produce, the baby-cheek feel of a ball of dough, the sigh of a quiche settling on the counter, the stray bits of cheese that you pop into your mouth, or the smell of butter turning nutty in the pan. There is the pleasure of good company, chatting while you chop, sitting down to a home-cooked meal with friends, and taking the time to savor, talk, laugh, and linger in the sated afterglow. And there is the pleasure of self-sufficiency, too, cooking something delicious just for yourself, setting the table for one, or curling up in a squashy chair with a tray on your lap and a book in your hand.

Cooking has an exhilarating way of being both an intimate activity — you follow your own appetite and play your own game, surrounded by your own happy chaos — and a universal one, as you submit yourself to forces greater than you, and walk in the footsteps of generations of cooks before you.

But I have met and held the hand of too many people who suffer from the infamous Kitchen Performance Anxiety syndrome, who feel overwhelmed by so many trendy recipes, pressured to try something new and fabulous at every meal, and threatened in their own sense of self if what comes out of the oven is anything short of sublime. It's great to nudge yourself out of your comfort zone, as that's how you'll grow as a cook, but don't take things (or yourself) too seriously: play with your food, and do whatever feels right and enjoyable. Something humble and simple, whipped up lightheartedly, will always taste better than an elaborate dish prepared by a stressed-out, cranky cook.

LES COURSES/FOOD SHOPPING

It would take a lot to distract me from the opportunity of exploring an unfamiliar food store and delving into the treasures it has to offer, peering through the glass cases, picking things up from shelves and putting them back, trying to figure out what everything is, and what I could do with it. I usually emerge after what feels like hours, loaded with bags that I happily lug home and unpack, filling my kitchen with edible wonders. Or sometimes I just revel in the observation and come out empty-handed but refreshed and inspired.

I also cherish the daily routine of dropping by my neighborhood shops, browsing through their usual array of products, and noticing what's new or just a bit different. I particularly enjoy the relationship that develops between you and the food vendors you visit regularly: the look of recognition as you step inside and the door gaily tinkles, how they remember what you bought last time, how they get you things from their private stash in the back, and how gladly they will share advice when they see your eagerness to listen, learn, and discuss the finer points of a superior lamb stew.

Thinking Seasonally

Fruits and vegetables simply taste better and cost less when they're in season and plentiful, when they've been grown reasonably close to you (thus avoiding the ordeal of refrigerated planes and trucks), and picked recently. True enough, this means that the winter months are a tad drearier than the warmer ones, but I like to follow this principle anyway: it keeps you in touch with the natural rhythm of the year, it builds up a sense of anticipation for the change of season, and you get to enjoy your food at its most sensuous peak of ripeness.

And it's not just produce that follows a yearly pattern. In France, there are laws that regulate the hunting, so fresh game is only available during the official hunting season, between September and January; outside of that period, it's either frozen, or illegal. Artisanal cheese is also a highly seasonal item, governed by the reproduction cycles of the animals, and the aging process that each variety requires.

At the farmer's market I frequent, the goat cheese stall disappears at the end of the winter, when the lady farmer is busy helping her goats give birth to kids. She returns a few weeks later with the creamiest mounds of goat cheese, which we scoop up hungrily. And when fall comes around and the milk production dwindles, she is left with a selection of more mature rounds of cheese, sharp and brittle but equally prized. Mountain cheeses also have a different personality according to when they were produced, since the flavor of the milk depends on what the cows were fed — fresh summer grass up on the mountain pastures or dried hay in the winter stables.

Finding the Best Sources

The grocery store may be the most convenient place to shop, but for many ingredients it isn't the best bet, and you're often left to your own devices to decide what to buy. If you have a farmer's market nearby, it is worth your time to go there for produce: the selection will be varied, fresh, and seasonal, and you will benefit from the knowledge of the vendors. The same thing goes if you have access to a bakery, a cheese shop, a fish market, or a butcher shop.

Organic, natural, and specialty foods stores also sell items that you can't find elsewhere, and not everything there is overpriced. As for ethnic markets, they are excellent sources for uncommon goods that will spike up your cooking, and they usually have a brisk turnover on a variety of grains, nuts, and spices.

Being Flexible

A recipe is a guide, not an absolute formula, and many substitutions can be made without any harm, using what's available, cheaper, or more to your taste. The easiest option is to keep within the same family of ingredients (nuts are often interchangeable, as are hard cheeses, leafy greens, stone fruits, etc.), but resources abound to offer more elaborate tips — *The Food Lover's Companion* and the *Cook's Thesaurus* (foodsubs.com) are particularly helpful.

My best food shopping strategy is to just go out, choose whatever looks fresh, and figure out later what to do with it. This makes the shopping much more exciting and spontaneous, and gives it a peculiar sense of freedom. The flip side is that I have to be careful not to buy too much, factoring in what I already have in stock. But if I do get carried away and come home with enough food to feed a small army, I can always call the soup pot and the freezer to the rescue, or invite a small army to dinner.

Where This Parisian Girl Gets Her Stuff

There are many romantic notions going around about the French and their food shopping ways. I would love to tell you that yes indeed, we all meet at the market every morning with our lopsided berets and our hand-woven wicker baskets, but the truth is that every household has its own routine, depending on where its members live and work, what stores they have access to, and whether they have the luxury and inclination to care about what they eat. While I can't speak for every one of my fellow countrymen, this is what food shopping looks like for someone who lives in Paris and cares passionately about the contents of her plate.

On Saturday mornings, when I manage to get up and ready before noon, I walk to the greenmarket on Boulevard des Batignolles for produce, cheese, and flowers. It is an organic open-air farmer's market, not too big and not too crowded, where most stall-keepers are indeed farmers. (In many other markets, they are simply retailers, who sell what they buy at the central market of Rungis, outside of Paris.)

At this market I find fruits and vegetables that are difficult or impossible to find anywhere else: heirloom varieties of cherries, forgotten vegetables, funky greens, unusual herbs . . . More often than not I'll be offered a sliver of something to taste, a pearl of wisdom on how to cook what I've purchased, or a bargain price on bruised fruits that will nonetheless make great compotes and jams.

There are a few excellent cheese stalls, too: a tiny one that sells goat cheese only, and another one with a wider selection, for which it is worth braving the line and the teasing of the vendor. As for the flower stand, it sells out fast — the flowers are very fresh and very cheap — so I go there as soon as I arrive, but the lady holds on to my tulips while I go about the rest of my shopping unencumbered.

Besides the market, my food sources of choice are the small stores that line the shopping streets near me, rue des Abbesses, rue Lepic, and rue des Martyrs. Each shop has a specialty — produce, cheese, meat, fish, wine, bread — and for each kind there are several to choose from, often just a few steps from one another. Over time I have selected my favorites, based on the quality and price of their products, and, just as important, the friendliness of their service: make me feel welcome, point me to the best options, throw a smile into the mix, and I'll be your loyal customer forever.

Most of these shops are family-owned — the butcher cuts your meat while his wife rings it up at the register — and I know how hard they work to keep their businesses afloat, threatened as they are by the many grocery stores around them. I have a lot of respect for their dedication and skill, and I see how essential they are to the life of the neighborhood. So while many consider the supermarket to be more convenient (and, admittedly, often cheaper), I am happy to make the choice of quality and support my local artisans as much as possible. (The only problem with the food shops around me is that they sit side-by-side with small designer-clothing stores, so that I might go out for a chicken and come back with a cute dress and a chicken.)

Beyond the daily needs that my neighborhood stores fill, I also love trekking around the city on a treasure hunt for specific items: chocolate, pastries, spices, exotic goods, baking supplies in bulk, hard-to-find ingredients . . . I ask around for recommendations, read the local press, and keep my eyes peeled when I walk down unfamiliar streets, hoping to stumble upon a hidden gem.

And when I travel in France or abroad, food shopping is my preferred angle of exploration. I do a little research beforehand to learn about the local specialties and bring back as many edibles as will possibly fit in my luggage. This usually means I can hardly lift said luggage, and my clothes may smell faintly of curry when I unpack, but it is a unique way to prolong the pleasures of travel, and my friends seem to be much more excited by these souvenirs than by snow globes.

I love taking tours of other people's pantries if they'll let me, so it's only fair I offer you a glimpse into mine.

DRY GOODS FOR BAKING. Several types of flour (all-purpose, whole wheat, chestnut, chickpea, buckwheat), sweeteners (granulated sugar, unrefined cane sugar, *vergeoise brune* [a moist beet sugar from Belgium], confectioners' sugar, *sucre perlé* [coarse pearls of sugar], molasses, different kinds of honey, fruit and flower syrups), and chocolate ingredients (cocoa powder, bittersweet chocolate, chocolate chips, roasted cacao nibs). Nuts (hazelnuts, almonds, pine nuts, pistachios, walnuts) and dried fruits (apricots, raisins, prunes, figs). Pure vanilla extract, baking powder, baking soda, dry yeast, agar-agar, cornstarch, candied ginger and orange peel, unsweetened grated coconut, poppy seeds, and toasted lemon zest.

Stocking your pantry

DRY GOODS FOR COOKING. Different kinds of pasta (short, long, spaetzle [egg noodles from Alsace]), rice (short-grain, long-grain, risotto), and grains (bulgur, quinoa, buckwheat). Green lentils from the Puy, dried white beans (*haricots Tarbais,* flageolets, or *cocos de Paimpol*), polenta, couscous, coarse chestnut meal, homemade bread crumbs, dried mushrooms, and sun-dried tomatoes.

CANNED AND JARRED GOODS. Whole peeled tomatoes, duck and goose products (foie gras, confit, gizzards), meat or fish or vegetable pâtés for impromptu apéritifs, different kinds of jams and savory confits, *crème de marron* (sweet chestnut paste), tuna, and sardines. Roasted bell peppers and *piquillos* (spicy bell peppers from the Basque country), artichoke hearts, olives, anchovies, capers, snails, homemade cornichons (pickled gherkins), and preserved lemons.

SPICE RACK. Herbes de Provence, thyme, rosemary, bay leaves, cumin seeds, coriander seeds, Spanish smoked paprika, peppercorns (black and pink), *piment d'Espelette* (ground and whole), mustard seeds, curry powder, and ras el hanout (a Moroccan spice mix). Cinnamon (ground and in sticks), whole nutmegs, whole cloves, French four-spice mix (cinnamon, cloves, ginger, nutmeg), and lavender. Different types of salt (fine sea salt, fleur de sel, coarse gray salt, flavored salts).

OIL, VINEGAR, ETC. Several kinds of oil (olive, walnut or hazelnut, sesame), vinegar (balsamic, cider, red wine, raspberry, poppy), and mustard (plain Dijon, old-fashioned with whole mustard seeds, purple mustard from Brives, tarragon mustard). Ketchup, Worcestershire sauce, dry white wine for cooking.

SEMIFRESH OR FRESH. Onions, shallots, and garlic. Several kinds of fresh herbs on the windowsill (thyme, basil, tarragon, whatever will grow in the Paris climate). And in the fridge: fresh cheese, extra-aged cheese (Parmesan, Comté, or Gouda), butter, eggs, cream, plain yogurt, and milk.

Simplicité

SIMPLICITY

You know how it is. Whenever you're at a party with people you don't know, someone is bound to pop the question, "So, what do you do?" I have to say I expand upon the subject with infinitely more animation now that my work matches my inner wants and needs, and when I do, my interlocutor unfailingly turns to Maxence with twinkling eyes to exclaim, "Wow, it must be an endless display of gastronomic prowess at your place!"

Full disclosure: not really. We eat well, that much is true, fresh vegetables from the greenmarket and quality goods from the shops around us, but the day-to-day menus are simple, and on weeknights we rely heavily on what we call picnic dinners: a bit of cheese from the cheese shop, a modest selection from the charcuterie, or leftover bits and pieces from the previous day's cooking. Add a hunk of bread from the bakery, a green salad or a bowl of soup, and you've got yourself a quickly assembled and heartily enjoyed meal.

And on other nights, when inspiration propels me into the kitchen, it's with an ample measure of improvisation that I cook, rummaging through the contents of the fridge, and putting together dishes that capture the day's mood and weather. This section holds a few favorites for simple meals, around which I'll weave variations to use what's on hand.

Salades

SALADS

Salade de Poulet, Pêches & Noisettes
CHICKEN SALAD WITH PEACHES AND HAZELNUTS

Salade de Haricots Verts, Noix de Pécan
& Jambon Cru
GREEN BEAN SALAD WITH PECANS
AND DRY-CURED HAM

Salade de Mâche, Clémentines & Thon Poêlé
MÂCHE SALAD WITH CLEMENTINES
AND SEARED TUNA

Salade Tiède de Haricots Blancs au
Pesto de Noix & Roquette
WARM BEAN SALAD WITH WALNUT-ARUGULA PESTO

SALADE DE POULET, PÊCHES & NOISETTES

Chicken Salad with Peaches and Hazelnuts

When I still worked in an office — before I joined the pajama workforce — I often brought my own lunch. It was a habit I had formed when I lived in the States and this was a widespread custom: I would join my coworkers in the bright orange company kitchen, and we would munch on our respective meals over a game of Boggle (I never once won, but it did enrich my English vocabulary with three- and four-letter words).

At my French office it was less common, and most of my colleagues walked to a nearby bistro for the *plat du jour*. This was quite pleasant and I joined them from time to time to catch up on office gossip, but for reasons of nutrition, cost, and variety, I still enjoyed putting together my little picnic in the morning.

In the summer, I liked to pack colorful salads and escape to the nearby Parc Montsouris at lunchtime. As I entered the park I would pass by a gastronomic restaurant set in a handsome pavilion and pore over the daily menu in lieu of an appetizer. I would walk on to sit by the little lake, where a handful of ducks swam about, in the vague hope that someone might throw stale bits of baguette their way.

A fork in my right hand, a book in the left, and the container of salad propped up against me with my left wrist — a technique that took years to refine — I would dig in happily, comfortable in my delicious solitude. And after a little post-lunch walk I would return to the office, refreshed and sated.

TOASTING NUTS revives their flavor and crunch, and the easiest way to do so is on the stovetop. Place the nuts in a single layer in a dry skillet. Set over medium-high heat and cook until fragrant and golden, 3 to 5 minutes, shaking the pan frequently. Remove the nuts from the skillet immediately, or they will continue to brown. For hazelnuts, it is also recommended to remove their brown skin: pour them from the skillet on a kitchen towel, gather the towel into a bundle, and let rest for 5 minutes. Rub the hazelnuts with the towel to remove as much skin as you can, and collect the nuts from the towel, discarding the skins.

This salad is a staple from those days, and I still prepare it now for quick lunches, simple dinners, or party buffets. It is an excellent use for leftover roasted chicken, which I like to buy at a rotisserie on rue des Abbesses, where the farm-raised chickens are plump and delectable, and where the lady looks strikingly like the famous French actress Marie-Anne Chazel.

1. Peel the peaches: this is easier if you blanch them first by putting them in a pan of simmering water for a minute. (If you use nectarines, it is unnecessary to peel them.)

2. In a medium salad bowl, whisk together the oil and vinegar. Add the chicken, peaches, hazelnuts, and cilantro. Season with salt and pepper, and toss to coat. Add the spinach leaves and toss again. Taste and adjust the seasoning. Serve immediately, or refrigerate for up to a day; it gets better as it sits. Remove from the fridge half an hour before eating.

NOTE If you prepare the salad in advance, the vinegar will wilt the greens a little. It will still taste good, but may not look as presentable: if you make it ahead for company, add the spinach at the last minute.

VARIATION Use fresh (or dried) apricots and almonds instead of peaches and hazelnuts.

*W*INE WEIN & SEKTGUT THIELEN MERLEN FETTGARTEN 2003 RIESLING SPATLESE (Germany, Mosel-Saar-Ruwer, white) A light-bodied wine with stone fruit flavors that reinforce the peach in the salad. Excellent balance between sweetness, to complement the slightly bitter nuts, and acidity, to stand up to the balsamic vinegar.

3 ripe yellow peaches, about 7 ounces each (substitute yellow nectarines)

3 tablespoons hazelnut oil (substitute walnut oil or extra virgin olive oil)

2 tablespoons balsamic vinegar

1 pound cooked chicken meat cut into strips, from a store-bought rotisserie chicken or a home-roasted chicken, about 3 cups

$2/3$ cup shelled hazelnuts, toasted, husked, and roughly chopped (see page 6)

$1/2$ cup (loosely packed) fresh cilantro leaves (substitute fresh flat-leaf parsley leaves)

Fine sea salt and freshly ground pepper

8 cups (packed) baby spinach leaves, about 8 ounces

❈

*Serves 4 as a main course,
6 to 8 as a starter*

SALADE DE HARICOTS VERTS, NOIX DE PÉCAN & JAMBON CRU

Green Bean Salad with Pecans and Dry-Cured Ham

My favorite Sunday lunch as a child was my mother's roasted chicken, served with sautéed potatoes and steamed green beans, topped with a dab of sweet butter. An important step of the preparation was the trimming of these beans, fresh from the morning market run, and we all took part in it. Around eleven, we would hear my mother's call from the kitchen, *"Il y a des haricots verts à éplucher!"*

Some might have grumbled at the chore, but I saw it as a welcome respite from the homework I was usually trying to expedite on Sunday mornings. My father, my sister, and I would sit on the carpet around the coffee table and roll up our sleeves as my mother brought in a tray with the beans in their brown paper wrapping and a colander to receive the trimmed ones. We had all gotten pretty dexterous over the years: in a matter of minutes the paper bag was empty, the colander full, and the tray scattered with tiny green tips. I had no choice but to get back to work, dragging my feet and hoping lunch would be ready soon.

GREEN BEANS are in season from May until September. Choose slender beans, brightly colored, with no blemishes. They should be plump and crisp to the touch. Store in the vegetable drawer of the fridge, and use within 2 to 3 days.

When I make fresh green beans now I can't really count on a full team of skilled trimmers, but I still take pleasure in the task and its absorbing nature. My fingers busy themselves instinctively — much like those of people who knit without looking — while I let my mind wander, thinking about the rest of the menu, our plans for the weekend, and whether I should cut my hair.

In this salad, trimming the beans is the only step that requires a bit of work. Sweet-talk someone into giving you a hand, or just embrace the process and its snapping sound track: the sprightly flavor and proud crispness of fresh green beans are worth your efforts.

1. Steam the beans for 10 minutes (12 if they are frozen), until cooked through but still crisp (if your steamer is small, work in two batches to ensure even cooking). Dump the beans in a large bowl of ice-cold water, to stop the cooking and preserve the beans' color. Drain thoroughly.

2. In a medium salad bowl, whisk together the oil and vinegar. Season with a little salt — not too much, as dry-cured ham is quite salty — and a generous grind of pepper. Add the beans and parsley, and toss gently to coat. Taste and adjust the seasoning. Arrange the ham and pecans over the beans. Serve immediately, or refrigerate for up to a day. Remove from the fridge half an hour before eating. (You can also plate the salad individually: divide the beans among plates, and top with ham and pecans.)

VARIATIONS Use sugar snap peas instead of green beans, or walnuts instead of pecans.

*W*INE JOSEPH DROUHIN 2004 BEAUJOLAIS VILLAGES (France, Burgundy, red) Beaujolais is always a successful match to ham. This wine is fruity and light, and its acidity is a great foil to salads. It has a nose of raspberry, cherry, and strawberry; its soft palate offers similar flavors, with a hint of earthiness that echoes the pecans.

$1^1/2$ pounds fresh green beans, trimmed (substitute frozen — no need to thaw them — but not canned)

2 tablespoons extra virgin olive oil

1 tablespoon cider vinegar

Fine sea salt and freshly ground pepper

$1/3$ cup (loosely packed) fresh flat-leaf parsley leaves, roughly chopped

3 ounces dry-cured ham, thinly sliced and shredded in 1-inch strips (I like to use jambon d'Ardèche, but prosciutto, Parma, or Serrano ham will work just as well)

$1/3$ cup pecans, toasted and roughly chopped (see page 6)

❀

Serves 4 as a main course, 6 to 8 as a starter

SALADE DE MÂCHE, CLÉMENTINES & THON POÊLÉ

*Mâche Salad with Clementines
and Seared Tuna*

 $\mathscr{I}$ am one of those people who crave the freshness of salads whatever the season. Assembling them doesn't take much forethought in the summertime, when the whole content of the greenmarket seems ready to jump straight into your salad bowl, but if you look closely, the colder months also offer plenty of produce to play with — mushrooms, root vegetables, citrus, pears, or young winter greens.

Mâche is a much loved salad green in France: while it isn't the most commonly consumed — the butterhead lettuce holds the title — it is prized for its succulent bouquets of tiny, spoon-shaped leaves. And since it grows best at low temperatures, it is conveniently at its peak during the winter.

To defy the dreary weather, I pay special attention to the colorfulness of my winter salads, and usually include a warm component added just before serving: toasts of roasted goat cheese (especially Rocamadour), spice-rubbed and grilled chicken, or perhaps sautéed duck gizzards, which we always have on hand — Maxence's grandparents live in the Périgord, and whenever we visit we can't help bringing back truckloads of canned duck products.

TUNA Since the tuna is cooked rare in this recipe, use super-fresh, high-quality fish. It should give off a fresh ocean smell, and feel firm to the touch — I have yet to meet a fishmonger who will let you fondle his products or stick your nose in them, but still, it's good to know what you're looking for. 🌿

In this mâche salad, the element of warmth is brought to you by cubes of fresh tuna: rolled in poppy seeds and briefly pan-seared, the fish offers a pleasing contrast between its black, crusty exterior and its meaty, tender flesh. Clementines round the dish with sweet acidulated notes, and a bright orange smile.

1. Rinse the mâche carefully (there may be a bit of sand at the roots) and spin it dry. Leave the bunches whole if the roots are clean and tender; trim them otherwise.

2. Squeeze the juice from a clementine — this should yield about 3 tablespoons juice. In a medium salad bowl, whisk together the clementine juice, balsamic vinegar, parsley, and the tablespoon of olive oil. Season with salt and pepper.

3. Peel the remaining clementines and separate them into segments. Pick any strand of pith from the segments. (If you use tangerines and the segments are large, cut them in half or thirds lengthwise.)

4. Pat the tuna dry with paper towels. Pour the poppy seeds in a shallow soup plate and dip the fish in to coat all sides, pressing gently so the seeds will adhere. Toss the mâche with the prepared dressing and arrange on plates.

5. Heat the 2 teaspoons olive oil in a large nonstick skillet over high heat. Place the fish in the skillet and cook for 1 minute on each side, until the surface is opaque but the flesh inside is still rare. Season with salt and pepper. Transfer the slices onto a cutting board and cut in cubes, working quickly so the fish won't get cold. Top each plate with tuna and clementine segments, and serve immediately.

10 cups mâche salad, about 8 ounces (also marketed as corn salad or lamb's lettuce; substitute watercress or baby spinach)

5 small and juicy clementine oranges, about 14 ounces (substitute tangerines)

2 teaspoons balsamic vinegar

2 tablespoons finely chopped fresh flat-leaf parsley leaves

1 tablespoon plus 2 teaspoons extra virgin olive oil

Fine sea salt and freshly ground pepper

2 steaks of fresh sushi-grade ahi tuna, also called yellowfin tuna, about $3/4$ inch thick, about 1 pound total

$1/4$ cup poppy seeds

Serves 4 as a light entrée, 6 as a starter

VARIATIONS To add a smoky flavor to the tuna, combine 2 teaspoons sweet Spanish smoked paprika (see page 29) with the poppy seeds. In the spring, use mixed young greens instead of mâche, and roasted strawberries in place of clementines: roast a pint of small hulled strawberries for 5 to 8 minutes in a 350°F oven, crush a few for the dressing, and top the salad with the remaining berries.

*W*INE CHÂTEAU DE MONTFORT VOUVRAY 2003 (France, Loire, white) Light-bodied and crisp, this Vouvray offers flavors of white peach and orange zest. It is mineral and slightly floral, with a fresh zing of tartness and acidity.

Salade de Mâche, Clémentines & Thon Poêlé
Mâche Salad with Clementines and Seared Tuna, page 10

Salade Tiède de Haricots Blancs au Pesto de Noix & Roquette
Warm Bean Salad with Walnut-Arugula Pesto, page 14

SALADE TIÈDE DE HARICOTS BLANCS AU
PESTO DE NOIX & ROQUETTE

Warm Bean Salad with Walnut-Arugula Pesto

*W*hite beans ranked high on my black list of foods all through my childhood and teenage days. My mother never served beans at home — she didn't like them either — so the only way I'd ever tried them was at the school cafeteria, where they were skillfully and consistently cooked into a mushy, mealy mess.

But when I started to get interested in cooking, one of my self-appointed missions was to reconsider all the ingredients I thought I hated: I would look for promising recipes, give them my best shot, and see if my taste buds might change their mind. Much to my glee, the list dwindled down to just a handful of items. And when it came to beans, I discovered that mush was not their only destiny, that dried beans were infinitely preferable to canned, and that it was worth driving across the country for a good plate of *cassoulet* — white beans slow-cooked with meat, a specialty from the southwest of France.

The variety I like best is a white bean called *haricot Tarbais*. It is grown around the city of Tarbes at the foot of the French Pyrenees and has a remarkably thin skin and smooth flesh — just what you hope to achieve after a day at the spa. Its culture was all but abandoned in the sixties, for it is a headstrong plant that resists mechanical harvesting, but it made a comeback in the eighties, when a group of local farmers started lobbying for its proper recognition, and for a denomination of origin.

These beans were born to be in a cassoulet and they make a stellar side to a roasted leg of lamb, but I like how this simple, warm salad reveals their nuttiness: the beans are cooked until just tender, so they will retain their shape and dignity, then coated with a bright, pestolike dressing of walnuts and arugula.

Since Tarbais beans are hand harvested and produced in such small quantities, they are not cheap and can be considered something of a luxury, but I am happy to report that this recipe yields excellent results with more humble breeds of white beans.

1. Soak the beans in 3 cups cold water for 12 hours or overnight. Drain and transfer into a large saucepan with the bay leaves. Pour in cold water so the beans are covered by 2 inches and bring to a simmer over medium heat. Cover and cook for 45 minutes to an hour (or according to package instructions), until the beans are tender but not mushy. Check the water level from time to time, and add more if it runs a little low. Thirty minutes into the cooking, add $1\frac{1}{2}$ teaspoons of the salt. (The beans can be prepared up to a day ahead.)

2. While the beans are cooking, combine the walnuts, arugula (reserve a few leaves for garnish if desired), oil, lemon juice, shallot, and the remaining $\frac{1}{2}$ teaspoon salt in a food processor or in a mortar. Process or grind with a pestle until the mixture forms a pastelike dressing. (The dressing can be prepared up to a day ahead. It can also be used in potato or chicken salad, or as a sandwich spread.)

$1\frac{1}{2}$ cups dried white beans, picked through and rinsed

2 bay leaves

2 teaspoons fine sea salt

$\frac{1}{4}$ cup plus 2 tablespoons shelled walnut halves, toasted (see page 6)

$1\frac{1}{2}$ cups (packed) arugula, about 2 ounces

$\frac{1}{4}$ cup walnut oil (substitute extra virgin olive oil)

1 tablespoon freshly squeezed lemon juice

1 small shallot, peeled and roughly chopped

Serves 4 as a main course, 6 to 8 as a starter or side

3. Drain the beans and let cool for a minute. Pour the dressing into a salad bowl, add the beans, and toss gently to coat. Garnish with the reserved arugula and serve while still warm. The leftovers are just as good the next day, cold or gently reheated.

VARIATION The dressing can be made with dry-salted anchovies (about 10 fillets, rinsed) instead of — or in addition to — arugula. Omit the salt from the dressing then.

WINE DOMAINE DES CHÉZELLES 2004 TOURAINE SAUVIGNON BLANC (France, Loire, white) A medium-bodied wine, with an intense Sauvignon Blanc nose — citrusy, grassy, and herbal — and enough acidity to counteract the richness of the beans and walnuts.

Sandwiches

Sandwich de Dinde au Curry
CURRIED TURKEY SANDWICH

Pan Bagnat

Tartine de Champignons au Cantal
MUSHROOM AND CANTAL CHEESE TARTINE

Club Sandwich Sardine & Tomate
SARDINE AND TOMATO CLUB SANDWICH

SANDWICH DE DINDE AU CURRY

Curried Turkey Sandwich

*O*n the first morning Maxence and I awoke in our new Paris apartment, I dressed quickly and walked to the nearest bakery, just a block away. A few minutes later I returned with two *croissants au beurre* in a thin paper bag and a rather over-priced carton of orange juice from the downstairs convenience store.

Fumbling through our pyramid of boxes we unearthed plates and glasses, and sat down to our very first Montmartre breakfast. Eyeing my croissant with a touch of anxiety, I took a tentative bite off the tip, chewed on it reflectively for a few seconds, and breathed a sigh of relief. A flaky buttery shell encasing a soft and slightly elastic flesh — this was just what a good croissant should be, and it could be found right around the corner. "We are going to be happy here," we said, brushing crumbs from our lips.

Over the months we tasted our way through this bakery's offerings and established our top three: a dense flourless chocolate cake, an old-fashioned *chausson aux pommes* (apple turnover), and an outstanding multigrain baguette, pointy-tipped and crusty. I soon developed an addiction to their curried turkey sandwich, made on this very baguette, and it became my lunch option of choice when I emerged from the pool after my weekly morning swim, heavy-limbed and quite famished.

Unfortunately, they changed the recipe after a while, and although the bread is still just as good, the filling has gone south — and I don't mean Provence. The turkey has all but disappeared, displaced by hard-boiled eggs, and there aren't nearly enough of those plump raisins that complemented the curry flavor so well. But you don't just storm into a French bakery and demand why their product fails to meet your taste standards. You would be met with a glare so icy it would give you frostbite, and you would never dare step in again — an unfortunate development if this is your corner bakery and you largely subsist on bread. So I went ahead and came up with a recipe that replicates the original version: I just buy their baguette and fix my own sandwich.

1. Put the raisins in a cup, pour boiling water over to cover, and set aside.

2. Heat the olive oil in a small skillet over medium heat. Press a garlic clove through a garlic press (or finely mince it), add the pulp and juices to the olive oil, and cook for a few seconds, stirring constantly, until fragrant. Add the turkey, season with salt and pepper, cover, and cook for 3 to 4 minutes on each side, until cooked through and slightly browned (but not tough as a shoe). Let cool.

3. In a small mixing bowl, combine 2 tablespoons yogurt, the cheese, 1 teaspoon curry powder, and the lemon juice, and mix with a fork. Press (or finely mince) the remaining garlic clove and add the pulp and juices to the yogurt mixture. Add a little more yogurt if necessary to make the mixture creamy. Season with salt and pepper and mix again. Taste and adjust the seasoning, adding more curry powder if desired.

4. Cut the turkey in bite-size chunks and combine with the yogurt mixture (for extra flavor, add the cooking juices from the skillet). Drain the raisins and add them to the mixture.

2 tablespoons dark raisins

2 teaspoons extra virgin olive oil

2 garlic cloves — one to cook the turkey, one for the dressing

6 ounces uncooked turkey cutlet, pounded thin

Fine sea salt and freshly ground pepper

2 tablespoons to $1/4$ cup plain unsweetened yogurt or Greek-style yogurt

2 tablespoons fresh goat cheese, ricotta, or cream cheese

1 to 2 teaspoons curry powder

1 tablespoon freshly squeezed lemon juice

One 9-ounce multigrain baguette (substitute plain baguette, multigrain rolls, or ciabatta)

1 cup (packed) mixed greens, about 1 ounce

2 tablespoons (packed) fresh cilantro leaves

※

Serves 2 as a main course

5. Cut the baguette lengthwise to get two equal half-baguettes. Slice each half open horizontally, not quite reaching the other side. Line the bottom with greens. Spread the turkey filling over the greens, dividing it equally between the two sandwiches, and sprinkle with cilantro. Close the sandwiches and serve immediately, or wrap tightly and refrigerate for a few hours, until half an hour before eating.

VARIATIONS Add tiny chunks of fresh pineapple or toasted sliced almonds; use seitan or smoked tofu instead of turkey; substitute dried apricots, diced, for the raisins.

Wine PIERRE SPARR, 2003 ALSACE ONE (France, Alsace, white) The fruitiness of this blend underlines the raisins with melon and pear flavors, but it is zesty and lemony enough to handle the curry. Serve well chilled.

PAN BAGNAT

*C*alling a sandwich "wet bread" — this is what *pan bagnat* means in the Nice dialect — is probably not the best marketing move, but let's shoo away any images of soggy sandwiches left in the cooler for too long. The bread here is not moistened by the bottle of water you've failed to close properly, but by liberal amounts of olive oil and the sweet juices seeping from ripe tomatoes.

Pan bagnat is basically a *salade Niçoise* in a bun, and it takes just a bite to understand why this sandwich, chock-full of summer flavors, is such a cherished child of Provençal cuisine. Originally intended as a snack for fishermen and early-morning workers, it called for cheap, plentiful ingredients and bread that didn't need to be very fresh, since it would have mopped up the juices and regained its senses by lunchtime.

Like many specialties that have traveled far beyond their original birthplace, pan bagnat is regularly abused and misinterpreted, at least from the perspective of purists. They advocate that the authentic recipe includes anchovies (tuna is accepted, but with pursed lips, as it was an expensive ingredient until the early twentieth century) and raw vegetables only. In addition to tomatoes and onions, our council of certified purists will let us use mixed young greens, young artichoke hearts, cucumbers, young fava beans, green bell peppers, scallions, and radishes. But grilled or otherwise cooked vegetables will not do. And whatever happens, mayonnaise is strictly prohibited (insert righteous shudder here).

Pan bagnat is the ideal sandwich for a picnic or a packed lunch, as it is meant to sit for a while before you eat it; the flavors will get to know each other, make conversation, and discover how much they have in common.

1. Slice the loaves in two horizontally. Drizzle the insides of each loaf, top and bottom, with olive oil. Core the tomatoes, slice them thinly (don't discard the juice or seeds), and arrange them on the bottom half of each loaf. Press the garlic cloves through a garlic press (or finely mince them), and spread the pulp and juices over the tomatoes. Season with a little salt, plenty of pepper, and a dash of vinegar. Top with the scallions, egg, if using, olives, anchovies, and basil. Arrange the greens over the filling, and cover with the tops of the loaves.

2. Wrap tightly in plastic and let sit somewhere cool (the gentle coolness of a cellar is preferable, but the refrigerator will be fine) for 2 to 12 hours before eating. Bring to room temperature before eating.

*W*INE MASI MASIANCO PINOT GRIGIO-VERDUZZO 2004 (Italy, Friuli–Venezia Giulia, white) This wine is crisp and fresh like most Pinot Grigio, with an acidity that responds to the tomatoes. Its citrusy and mineral flavors accent the briny anchovies and olives, while the local Verduzzo grape brings complexity and a smooth mouthfeel.

2 round loaves good-quality soft white bread, 4 to 5 inches in diameter, such as focaccia (baguette is untraditional, but works well, too)

Extra virgin olive oil

2 medium tomatoes

2 garlic cloves

Fine sea salt and freshly ground pepper

Red wine vinegar

2 scallions, trimmed and sliced thinly

1 large hard-boiled egg, peeled and sliced (optional)

8 medium black olives such as Kalamata, pitted and sliced in halves — buy olives in bulk or jarred, not canned

4 ounces dry-salted anchovies packed in salt or olive oil, rinsed and patted dry if packed in salt, and cut in halves (substitute 4 ounces canned tuna packed in olive oil, drained well)

8 fresh basil leaves, torn into strips

1 cup (packed) mixed greens

Serves 2 as a main course
Resting time: 2 hours

Sandwich de Dinde au Curry
Curried Turkey Sandwich, page 18

Pan Bagnat, page 20

Tartine de Champignons au Cantal
Mushroom and Cantal Cheese Tartine, page 24

TARTINE DE CHAMPIGNONS AU CANTAL

Mushroom and Cantal Cheese Tartine

$\mathscr{T}$he original meaning of the word *tartine* (tar-teen) is a simple slice of bread that one spreads with butter, jam, or cheese for breakfast or a quick snack. But in recent years, the tartine concept has evolved into a popular main dish, often featured in casual Parisian restaurants. This second-generation tartine consists of a large slice of bread topped with savory ingredients in a sort of open-face sandwich — I like to think of it as a nod to the Middle Ages, when slices of bread were used in lieu of plates.

CANTAL CHEESE *is one of the most ancient French cheeses: its production dates back to the first century* A.D. *It is a semifirm cow's milk cheese from Auvergne, a mountainous region in the heart of France. Pleasantly pasty in texture, it is fruity and nutty, with a slight sharpness. It fares well in shavings or cubes over a salad, and it melts beautifully for a cheese fondue, or on this tartine. Salers is a close cousin, and a happy substitute. If you can't find either, use another semifirm or firm mountain cheese, such as Tomme, Beaufort, or Comté.* ❦

Such a flexible idea is open to an infinite number of variations, but it should be used with caution and a sound combination of ingredients: whipping up a tartine with random leftovers from the fridge can work wonders — or not. It's also tempting to throw in lots of goodies (the more, the merrier) but as the golden rule of cooking goes, too many flavors will cancel each other out.

The quality of the bread is decisive: peasant-style loaves (such as *pain Poilâne*, the artisanal levain bread from Paris' world-famous bakery) are the most commonly used, but you can use any other sort of bread, as long as it's fresh and flavorful. Ideally, the inside of the bread should be tightly knit so the ingredients won't fall through the holes. The thickness of the slices varies, but a third or half an inch is a good size, and you can toast the bread to crisp it up if you like. The bread is first lined with something moist (butter, tapenade, pesto, hummus, eggplant caviar, fresh cheese, or any type of cheese that will melt nicely in the oven) to coat it and keep the other ingredients in place as you arrange them on top in an attractive pattern.

Tartines can be served at room temperature or hot, after a few minutes under the broiler. You can set them on regular dinner plates, but they will look quite stylish on rectangular ones, or on small wooden cutting boards, like medieval trenchers. The classic accompaniment to tartines is a lightly dressed green salad, but I've seen them served with other vegetable sides, such as ratatouille (see page 138). In any case, it should be something light and simple that will match the ingredients of the tartine without drawing too much attention from it.

The following tartine is perfect for a quick dinner or brunch in the fall. The bread is topped with Cantal cheese and tender mushrooms, and these warm, earthy flavors are brightened up by fresh parsley and a hint of lemon zest.

1. Heat the 1 teaspoon olive oil in a medium skillet over medium-high heat. Add the minced garlic (reserve the second clove) and the shallots, and cook for 2 minutes, until softened, stirring regularly. Add the mushrooms and season with salt and pepper. Lower the heat to medium, cover, and cook for 3 minutes. Remove the lid and cook for 3 more minutes, until the juices have evaporated. Taste and adjust the seasoning.

2. Toast the bread lightly and rub with the cut sides of the remaining clove. Line a baking sheet with foil, grease the foil with 1 teaspoon oil, and preheat the oven on the broiler setting.

3. Cut the cheese in shavings using a vegetable peeler and arrange on the bread. Top with the mushroom mixture and transfer to the prepared baking sheet. Put under the broiler for 3 to 5 minutes, keeping an eye on them, until the cheese is melted. Sprinkle the tartines with chopped parsley and lemon zest, and serve immediately.

1 teaspoon extra virgin olive oil, plus 1 teaspoon for greasing foil

2 garlic cloves, one finely minced, one sliced in two

2 small shallots, thinly sliced

12 ounces fresh cremini mushrooms, stems cut off, brushed clean, and sliced (this will yield about 4 cups sliced)

Fine sea salt and freshly ground pepper

Two $^1/_2$-inch-thick large slices peasant-style bread, about $2^1/_2$ ounces each

$1^1/_2$ ounces Cantal (substitute Tomme, Beaufort, or Comté)

2 tablespoons roughly chopped fresh flat-leaf parsley leaves

1 teaspoon (loosely packed) finely grated lemon zest, from an organic lemon

Serves 2 as a main course

VARIATIONS Use a good Cheddar or Parmesan instead of Cantal, and try other kinds of mushrooms, such as cèpes or oyster mushrooms.

𝒲INE PERRIN RÉSERVE CÔTES DU RHÔNE ROUGE 2003 (France, Côtes du Rhône, red) A medium-bodied wine with a good tannin structure. It has a nose of black fruit and black pepper, with meaty and earthy overtones, and a slight tartness. A Burgundy would also be a good, albeit pricier, choice.

CLUB SANDWICH SARDINE & TOMATE

Sardine and Tomato Club Sandwich

𝒯here is something uniquely pleasing about the club sandwich: the whole double-decker idea is pure genius — it's like getting two sandwiches in one — and the triangular shape makes it a delight to eat. I bite off the crisp corners first, keeping the meaty middle for last, but this is a matter of personal preference.

The classic club sandwich is layered with bacon and chicken (sometimes turkey), tomato, lettuce, and mayonnaise, but I like to take the double-decker concept and run with it, inventing new formulas. In the following version, the bread is spread with fresh cheese and a chunky smoked tomato confit, then filled with sardines and arugula. Pungent and peppery, generous and moist, it is a blissful lunch.

1. Heat the oil in a small saucepan over medium heat. Add the shallots and garlic and cook for 2 minutes, until soft and fragrant, stirring regularly. Add the tomatoes, smoked paprika, salt, pepper, and sugar. Lower the heat to medium-low and cook for 30 minutes, uncovered, stirring from time to time, until the mixture is thick and the juices have evaporated. Transfer to a bowl to cool. (This can be prepared up to a day in advance. The tomato confit can also be mixed until smooth and used as a spread or dip.)

2. Drain the sardines and pat with paper towels to remove excess oil. Mash roughly with a fork and divide into four equal portions. Slice off and discard the crusts of the bread (or leave them out to dry for a day and mix in a blender to make bread crumbs), and toast the slices until golden brown.

3. Assemble the slices of bread into double-decker sandwiches, spreading each deck with fresh cheese and tomato jam, then filling it with sardines and arugula. Use a sharp bread knife to halve the sandwiches diagonally and secure each half with a toothpick if desired. Serve immediately, or wrap in wax paper and go eat on a patch of green somewhere.

*W*INE MARQUES DE ARIENZO 2001 CRIANZA RIOJA (Spain, Rioja, red) Rioja has a regional affinity with smoked paprika, and Crianza is a lighter-style Rioja that works well with the sardines. Its flavors are simple, mostly cherry, joined by lightly smoky and vanilla notes, and its acidity answers to the tomatoes.

1 tablespoon extra virgin olive oil

2 small shallots, finely minced

1 garlic clove, finely minced or pressed

One 14-ounce can whole tomatoes, drained and chopped

$1/4$ teaspoon sweet Spanish smoked paprika (see page 29; substitute chipotle pepper or smoked jalapeño flakes [hotter], or Hungarian paprika [milder])

$1/4$ teaspoon fine sea salt

$1/4$ teaspoon freshly ground pepper

$1/4$ teaspoon light brown sugar

One 3.75-ounce can good-quality sardines, packed in olive oil (substitute canned kipper or tuna)

6 large slices multigrain sandwich bread

$1/4$ cup fresh goat cheese, ricotta, or cream cheese

1 cup (packed) arugula (substitute mixed greens or baby spinach)

* * *

Serves 2 as a main course

Club Sandwich Sardine & Tomate
Sardine and Tomato Club Sandwich, page 26

Spanish Smoked Paprika

Spanish smoked paprika, or Pimentón de La Vera, is a specialty from Extremadura in the southwest of Spain. It is made from chile peppers slowly smoked over an oakwood fire and ground to a fine powder. It is a bold but versatile seasoning that comes in three degrees of heat: mild (*dulce*), as used in this recipe, medium (*agridulce*), or hot (*picante*). You can find it at Latin markets, or order it online. The true Pimentón de La Vera is protected by a denomination of origin — look for tins that state "Denominación de Origen."

Tartes Salées

SAVORY TARTS

Pâte Brisée
SHORT PASTRY

Quiche Oignon & Cumin
ONION AND CUMIN QUICHE

Tartelettes aux Poivrons Rouges & Pignons
RED PEPPER AND PINE NUT TARTLETS

Quiche de Broccoli à la Pomme
BROCCOLI AND APPLE QUICHE

Tarte Tatin à la Tomate
TOMATO TATiN

PÂTE BRISÉE

Short Pastry

French grocery stores offer plenty of shortcut options for the hasty quiche maker: puff or short pastry, pure butter or margarine, pre-rolled into a circle or shaped in a rectangular block, fresh or frozen . . . A store-bought pastry shell (available in the fresh or frozen foods section at most supermarkets in the U.S.) is a perfectly acceptable choice if you have no time or inclination to bake one from scratch. That's what I used in my savory tarts for years to no complaint, until I tried making my own short pastry: it turned out to be much easier than I'd expected, and all tasters agreed that the texture and flavor of a homemade crust made a real difference. I still use store-bought pastry in a pinch, but here is the recipe I use when I have time for fresh.

1¹/₃ cups all-purpose flour

¹/₂ teaspoon fine sea salt

8 tablespoons (1 stick) chilled unsalted butter, diced

1 large egg, lightly beaten

Ice-cold water

Makes enough dough for a 10-inch tart or quiche, or six 5-inch tartlets
Chilling time: 30 minutes

1. **If working with a food processor,** combine the flour, salt, and butter in the processor. Process at low speed for about 10 seconds, until the mixture resembles coarse meal. Add the egg and mix again for a few seconds, until the dough comes together into a ball. If the dough is still a little dry, add a little ice-cold water, 1 teaspoon at a time, and process again in short pulses until the dough comes together. Turn out on a lightly floured work surface, and gather into a ball without kneading. Proceed to step 2.

If working by hand, sift the flour into a medium mixing bowl. Add the salt and diced butter, and rub the mixture with the tips of your fingers or a wire pastry blender until the mixture resembles coarse meal. Beat the egg lightly in a small bowl. Form a well in the center of the flour mixture, add the egg, and blend it in gently with a fork. When most of the egg is incorporated, knead gently until the dough comes together. If it is a little dry, add ice-cold water, 1 teaspoon at a time, until the dough forms a ball. Avoid overworking the dough, or it will be tough. Proceed to step 2.

2. Shape the dough into a slightly flattened ball. Wrap tightly in plastic and refrigerate for 30 minutes, or up to a day. Let stand at room temperature before using, just long enough that the dough can be rolled out without cracking: this usually takes about 10 minutes, but it will vary depending on the heat and humidity. The dough can also be frozen for up to a month.

3. Sprinkle flour lightly on a clean work surface and on your rolling pin, and place the slightly flattened ball of dough on the work surface in front of you. Roll the pin over the dough two or three times with moderate pressure. Rotate the dough by a quarter of a turn clockwise and roll the pin over it two or three times. Repeat these steps until you get a circle large enough to line your pan, sprinkling the work surface and the rolling pin with a little more flour when the dough starts to stick to either of them.

VARIATIONS Flavor the dough with a tablespoon of dried herbs (rosemary, thyme, oregano), $1/2$ to 1 teaspoon ground spices (nutmeg, ginger, cumin), or $1/4$ cup grated hard cheese (Parmesan in particular). Add these flavorings with the flour.

QUICHE OIGNON & CUMIN

Onion and Cumin Quiche

𝒬uiches are a ubiquitous dish on French tables: we bake them at home for simple family meals, serve them at buffets and parties, or order them by the slice at casual, lunch-type restaurants, where the menu often includes a *quiche du jour*.

Strictly speaking, a quiche should have a custard filling — made with eggs, milk, cream, and sometimes cheese — but it belongs to the wider and equally popular category of savory tarts (*tartes salées*), in which a thick sauce or spread can replace the custard. I think of quiche as a comforting cold-weather dish, whereas custardless savory tarts hold more appeal during the summer months.

Beyond the classic and heavenly *quiche lorraine* — a simple custard with cubes of smoked bacon (*lardons*) — there are thousands of recipes out there, featuring different ingredients and pairings. I like to improvise with what's in season and in the fridge, but this golden onion quiche has earned me some of my best marriage proposals.

1. Prepare the Pâte Brisée. Wrap tightly in plastic and refrigerate for 30 minutes, or up to a day.

2. Heat 1 tablespoon olive oil in a large skillet over medium heat. Add the onions, sprinkle with ¼ teaspoon of the salt, and stir. Cover, turn the heat down to low, and cook for 30 minutes, stirring from time to time, until the onions are soft and translucent. Remove the lid, turn the heat to medium-high, and cook for another 5 minutes, stirring regularly, until most of the liquids have evaporated. (This can be prepared up to a day ahead.)

3. Remove the dough from the refrigerator and let stand at room temperature for 10 minutes before using. Preheat the oven to 350°F. Grease a 10-inch ceramic quiche pan with 1 teaspoon olive oil. Working on a lightly floured surface, roll out the dough

in a 12-inch circle. Transfer the dough into the pan, prick the bottom all over with a fork, and press on the sides with your fingers so the dough will adhere. Bake for 7 minutes, until lightly golden. Remove from the oven (leave the heat on) and set aside.

4. In a medium mixing bowl, whisk together the eggs and cream. Season with the remaining $1/4$ teaspoon salt, the pepper, and the cumin. Fold in the cheese and onions, and pour into the tart shell.

5. Bake for 35 minutes, until the top is golden and the center of the quiche is still slightly jiggly. Turn the oven off and leave the quiche in the closed oven for 10 minutes, until the filling is set. Serve warm, with a salad of butterhead lettuce. You can make the quiche a few hours or a day ahead and reheat it for 15 minutes in a 350°F oven to revive the crispness of the crust.

VARIATION Omit the cumin and add diced bacon or pancetta, sautéed until crisp.

*W*INE BORTOLOTTI PROSECCO BRUT NV (Italy, Veneto, sparkling white) A tasty and inexpensive bubbly wine. Its fresh acidity and citrusy notes accentuate the sweetness of the slow-cooked onions and balance the earthy cumin flavors.

Pâte Brisée (page 32; alternatively, you can use a sheet of uncooked store-bought puff pastry, thawed according to package instructions if frozen)

1 tablespoon extra virgin olive oil, plus 1 teaspoon for greasing the pan

2 pounds yellow onions, about 6 medium, thinly sliced

$1/2$ teaspoon fine sea salt

3 large eggs

$3/4$ cup light cream

$1/4$ teaspoon freshly ground pepper

2 teaspoons whole cumin seeds

$1^1/2$ cups freshly grated Comté, about 5 ounces (substitute Gruyère)

---

*Serves 4 to 6 as a main course, 8 to 10 as a starter
Chilling time: 30 minutes
for the dough*

Quiche Oignon & Cumin
Onion and Cumin Quiche, page 34

Tartelettes aux Poivrons Rouges & Pignons
Red Pepper and Pine Nut Tartlets, page 38

TARTELETTES AUX POIVRONS ROUGES & PIGNONS

Red Pepper and Pine Nut Tartlets

It took me years of gearing up before I finally dared roast my own bell peppers. I'd always loved roasted peppers, and I knew that freshly roasted tasted incomparably better than jarred; I'd read all about the different methods, about the tips and tricks, but I had never witnessed the process with my own eyes, and I held the irrational belief that it just would not work.

Sure, hundreds and thousands of other cooks were roasting peppers every day, but I couldn't imagine how *my* peppers, fresh and firm and plasticky to the touch, could ever turn into soft and supple versions of themselves, or how their skin could actually char and blister in my innocent oven. And as all brave people do when something frightens them, I stayed at a safe distance, and made do with jarred.

Until one day, feeling intrepid and audacious with two bell peppers in my fridge, I decided to give it a shot. It worked perfectly, of course. It was the easiest thing in the whole world — it was fun, even — and the resulting strips were so moist and flavorsome you would have sworn they'd been lavishly coated with the most aromatic of oils. Since then, I have joined the Club of Enthusiastic Bell Pepper Roasters (apply for membership today!), and these tartlets are one of the dishes I make with the fruits of my roasting. They can be made with jarred bell peppers if you're pressed for time, or scared.

1. Prepare the Pâte Brisée. Wrap tightly in plastic and refrigerate for 30 minutes, or up to a day.

2. Remove the stems from the roasted peppers, seed the peppers, and pat them dry with paper towels. Combine the roasted peppers, anchovies, and Tabasco in a food processor and purée until smooth. Taste and adjust the seasoning.

3. In a small skillet, combine the pine nuts with 2 teaspoons of the oil the anchovies were packed in (or olive oil if you use salt-packed anchovies) and toast until golden.

This will give them extra flavor and a nice, even color, but you can toast the pine nuts in a dry skillet if you prefer. (The roasted pepper spread and the pine nuts can be prepared up to a day ahead.)

4. Remove the dough from the fridge and let stand at room temperature for 10 minutes. Preheat the oven to 350°F and line a baking sheet with parchment paper. Divide the dough into six equal pieces. Working with one piece at a time, roll out the dough thinly on a lightly floured surface. Use an overturned bowl (5 to 6 inches in diameter) as a guide to cut out a disk of dough, running a sharp knife closely against the rim of the bowl. Arrange the six disks on the prepared baking sheet, prick all over with a fork, and bake for 15 minutes, watching them closely, until golden.

5. Remove the tartlets from the oven. Spread each of them with 2 rounded tablespoons of the roasted pepper mixture, leaving a thin margin all around. Sprinkle with pine nuts, fresh bell pepper dice, and parsley. Serve immediately with a salad of arugula or mixed greens, or cut in wedges for a fine appetizer.

Pâte Brisée (page 32; alternatively, you can use a sheet of uncooked store-bought puff pastry, thawed according to package instructions if frozen)

FOR THE FILLING

2 pounds red bell peppers, about 4 medium, home-roasted (see page 40), or one 14-ounce jar roasted red bell peppers, packed in water, drained

6 fillets dry-salted anchovies packed in salt or olive oil (reserve the oil), rinsed and patted dry if packed in salt (substitute 2 tablespoons salted capers, rinsed)

$1/2$ to 1 teaspoon Tabasco sauce

3 tablespoons pine nuts

Half a fresh red bell pepper, seeded and diced

2 tablespoons finely chopped fresh flat-leaf parsley leaves

❋

Serves 6 as a light main course or starter
Chilling time: 30 minutes for the dough

VARIATIONS Once you've spread the bell pepper purée on the tartlets, top with thinly sliced goat cheese and pop the tartlets back in the oven for a few minutes. The tartlets can also be made in miniature size: use a juice glass to cut out the disks of dough.

WINE TUE-BŒUF "LE BUISSON POUILLEUX" TOURAINE 2004 (France, Loire, white) An outstanding Sauvignon Blanc, unfiltered and funky. Its nose is dominated by ripe peach and the citrus aromas typical of the varietal. This impression carries over to the palate, joined by herbal, earthy notes and hints of pepper and spice.

Roasting Peppers **Roasting bell peppers takes a bit of time, but it is easy and the flavor is outstanding. There are different methods — over an open flame, with a kitchen torch, in a barbecue pit — but I do it in the oven. Start with 2 pounds red bell peppers, about 4 medium, firm and smooth skinned. Arrange the whole bell peppers on a baking sheet lined with foil and bake for 35 to 45 minutes at 400°F, turning the peppers every 10 minutes or so, until they are very soft and their skin has dark spots and blisters all over, poor things. Remove the baking sheet from the oven and close the foil over the peppers to form an airtight package (use an extra sheet of foil if necessary). Let stand for 15 minutes. Open the package and wait until the peppers are just cool enough to handle — I am an impatient person, and I usually burn the tips of my fingers. Pull out the stems and slice the bell peppers open. Scrape off the seeds and strings of membrane with a knife, and peel off the skin. Let cool and eat as is, add to sandwiches, salads, and pasta sauces, or use in this tartlet recipe. Roasted bell peppers will keep for a few days in the fridge; freeze for longer storage.**

QUICHE DE BROCCOLI À LA POMME

Broccoli and Apple Quiche

$\mathscr{I}$ first came up with this recipe after a greenmarket run one fall morning. In the tottering pile of goods I unloaded on my counter — I am always amazed at how much my shopping bag will hold — was a milky round of fresh goat cheese that had already dampened its paper wrapping, a dark emerald head of broccoli, and tiny apples that didn't look like much but tasted like candy.

All three ingredients were enrolled in a quiche for lunch, and it appeared that the company of cheese and fruit was quite flattering to the broccoli, offsetting its slight bitterness and making this dish my secret weapon to convert broccoli-loathing friends.

This recipe uses only the florets of broccoli, but don't discard the stems: trim the tough ends and add the rest to a soup, or grate it to make a salad with raisins and sunflower seeds, in a simple dressing of balsamic vinegar and olive oil.

1. Prepare the Pâte Brisée. Wrap tightly in plastic and refrigerate for 30 minutes, or up to a day.

2. Steam the broccoli florets for 7 minutes, until cooked but still firm. Set aside in a colander. In a medium mixing bowl, whisk together the milk, cream, and eggs. Season with salt, pepper, and nutmeg.

3. Remove the dough from the fridge and let stand at room temperature for 10 minutes. Preheat the oven to

Pâte Brisée (page 32; alternatively, you can use a sheet of uncooked store-bought puff pastry, thawed according to package instructions if frozen)

FOR THE FILLING

1 medium head broccoli, about 1^1/2 pounds, florets only, rinsed and cut in small chunks (about 6 cups florets)

^{1}/3 cup milk

^{1}/3 cup light cream

3 large eggs

^{1}/2 teaspoon fine sea salt

Freshly ground pepper

Freshly grated nutmeg

1 teaspoon olive oil for greasing the pan

1 medium baking apple or 2 small ones, about 7 ounces

4 ounces fresh goat cheese, cut in ^{1}/2-inch chunks

Serves 4 to 6 as a main course
Chilling time: 30 minutes for the dough

Quiche de Broccoli à la Pomme
Broccoli and Apple Quiche

350°F. Grease a 10-inch ceramic quiche pan with olive oil. Working on a lightly floured surface, roll out the dough in a 12-inch circle. Transfer the dough into the pan, prick the bottom all over with a fork, and press on the sides with your fingers so the dough will adhere. Bake for 7 minutes, until lightly golden.

4. Peel, quarter, core, and dice the apple. Remove the pan from the oven (leave the heat on). Arrange the broccoli, apple, and cheese in the tart shell. Pour in the milk mixture and bake for 35 minutes. Turn the oven off and leave the quiche in the closed oven for 10 more minutes, until the filling is set.

5. Transfer the pan to a rack to cool for 5 minutes. Serve warm, with a mâche salad. You can make the quiche a few hours or a day ahead and reheat it for 15 minutes in a 350°F oven to revive the crispness of the crust.

*W*INE DOMAINE TOLLOT-BEAUT 2000 BOURGOGNE WHITE BURGUNDY (France, Burgundy, white) Full-bodied but not oak-heavy, this wine displays ripe and roasted flavors of apple and pear, with hints of cinnamon, vanilla, and nutmeg. It has enough acidity to bring balance, which is crucial for egg dishes. It is rich but harmonious, with a clean finish.

TARTE TATIN À LA TOMATE

Tomato Tatin

*A*s someone who cherishes words just as much as food, christening my dishes is an important part of my cooking pleasure. I like to make sure that the name is simple — although I occasionally lapse into fancy restaurant style just for the fun of it — and that it hints at the composition but retains an element of fun or mystery. One of the naming tricks I favor is using a dessert name for a savory course, and vice versa. It gives the dish a playful persona, and points out the many bridges that can be crossed between the sweet and the savory.

This tomato tart is a glorious example: the tomatoes are topped with goat cheese and tapenade and cooked under a layer of pastry in classic tarte tatin fashion. This allows the filling to bake softly without drying out, and provides a bit of an adrenaline thrill when you have to flip the tart on a serving platter — don't worry, it will slip right out.

Pâte Brisée (page 32; alternatively, you can use a sheet of uncooked store-bought puff pastry, thawed according to package instructions if frozen)

FOR THE FILLING

Extra virgin olive oil

2 pounds Roma or plum tomatoes (substitute any other firm and not too juicy variety)

Fine sea salt and freshly ground pepper

Herbes de Provence (or a mix of dried rosemary, basil, oregano, and thyme)

1/4 cup black olive tapenade, store-bought or homemade (see page 79)

6 ounces fresh goat cheese

1/3 cup (loosely packed) fresh basil leaves

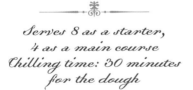

Serves 8 as a starter,
4 as a main course
Chilling time: 30 minutes
for the dough

1. Prepare the Pâte Brisée. Wrap tightly in plastic and refrigerate for 30 minutes, or up to a day.

2. Preheat the oven to 350°F and grease a 10-inch ceramic quiche pan with 1 teaspoon olive oil.

3. Halve the tomatoes lengthwise and core them. Run your thumb in the hollows of the tomatoes to remove the juice and seeds. Arrange in the pan, skin side down, in a circular pattern. You can crowd them a little; they will shrink as they bake. Season with salt, pepper, herbs, and a good drizzle of olive oil. Bake for 30 minutes, until softened. Remove from the oven (leave the heat on).

4. Remove the dough from the fridge and let stand at room temperature for 10 minutes. Working on a lightly floured surface, roll out the dough in an 11-inch circle and prick all over with a fork. Spread with tapenade, leaving a 1-inch margin all around.

5. Cut the cheese in 1/3-inch slices and arrange over the tomatoes in the pan. Lay the dough, tapenade side down, on the cheese, and tuck in the overhanging flaps of dough. Bake for 30 to 40 minutes, until the crust is golden.

6. Let cool for a few minutes on a rack. Run a knife around the crust to loosen. Put on your best-looking oven mitts, cover the pan with an overturned serving plate, and flip the whole thing carefully. If some of the tomatoes stick to the bottom of the pan,

Tarte Tatin à la Tomate
Tomato Tatin

just place them back on the tart where they belong. Serve warm or at room temperature. Just before serving, snip or tear the basil leaves and sprinkle over the tart.

VARIATIONS Instead of tapenade, spread the dough with onion confit, anchovy paste, or pesto (see page 80 to make your own pistachio pesto). Instead of goat cheese, use slices of buffalo mozzarella, drained and patted dry with paper towels.

*W*INE LA NUNSIO 2002 BARBERA D'ASTI (Italy, Piedmont, red) The acidity of this wine makes it very food-friendly. With its red and black fruit flavors, it is a straightforward (and very affordable) wine that fares well with simple tomato-dominant dishes.

Soupes

SOUPS

Soupe au Pistou
PISTOU SOUP

Soupe de Poulet Gratinée aux Baies Roses
GRATINÉED CHICKEN SOUP WITH
PINK PEPPERCORNS

Velouté de Châtaigne & Champignons
CHESTNUT AND MUSHROOM SOUP

*Soupe Glacée aux Pousses d'Épinard
& Crevettes*
BABY SPINACH AND SHRIMP CHILLED SOUP

SOUPE AU PISTOU

Pistou Soup

*P*istou is the Provençal equivalent of the Italian pesto, an explosive paste of basil, garlic, cheese, and olive oil, ground together with a mortar and pestle. While pistou can be used in much the same way as pesto, its true calling is this soup, simply called *soupe au pistou*. It is a beautiful vegetable soup, full of nuances, to which the pistou is added as a condiment at the table.

SHELLING BEANS *are what all dried beans used to be before they were, well, dried. They can be found in farmer's markets in the summer and fall, still in the pod. They need to be shelled, but they cook faster than dried beans. They are also sweeter and more tender, with a delicate nuttiness. Any variety will work for this soup (cranberry, lima, kidney); if you happen to find several kinds, you can mix and match.* ✿

Soupe au pistou was one of my grandmother's specialties when her health still allowed her to cook. My father loved it so much as a little boy that he was once caught in his pajamas by the open fridge, having gotten up at night to eat just a little more. I am now the proud owner of my grandmother's marble mortar, a venerable eight-pound beauty that she found in the garden of a house she and my grandfather rented in Marseille, back in 1937. Naturally, I am convinced that it imparts a special flavor to my pistou.

Soupe au pistou is traditionally served in the summer or early fall when basil, fresh beans, and tomatoes are at their peak, but you can also prepare it during the winter using dried beans, frozen green beans, and canned tomatoes. It is best made a day ahead, but the pistou should be freshly ground, if possible.

1. Heat the olive oil in a large soup pot. Add the onions and 1 tablespoon water to the pot. Cook over medium heat for 10 minutes, stirring regularly to avoid coloring, until soft and translucent. Add the rest of the vegetables, bay leaves, and thyme. Season with salt and pepper.

2. Pour boiling water to just cover the vegetables and bring to a simmer. Cover, lower the heat to medium-low, and simmer for 1½ hours, stirring regularly to make sure the vegetables don't stick to the bottom, and adding boiling water if it no longer covers the vegetables. After cooking for 1 hour and 20 minutes, add the macaroni and 1 cup boiling water and stir to combine. (The soup is best made a day ahead.)

3. Two hours or less before serving, prepare the pistou. Press the garlic cloves with a garlic press (or mince them finely) and combine the pulp and juices with the basil and grated cheese in a mortar. Grind into a paste with the pestle, adding olive oil little by little until the pistou forms a smooth paste. (This can also be done in a food processor, but the flavors won't be quite as stupendous and my grandmother won't be quite as proud of you.) Transfer into a serving cup.

4. Fish out the bay leaves and thyme sprigs from the soup, or just warn your guests not to eat them. Serve the soup hot or slightly warm, with pistou on the side for each diner to stir a spoonful into his bowl.

𝒲**INE** MAS DE GOURGONNIER ROSÉ 2003 (France, Provence, rosé) This wine has more complexity than you might expect from a rosé. It is lightly fruity (strawberry, kiwi, and citrus), with herbal green notes reminiscent of herbes de Provence. It offers a fresh acidity, with subtle hints of earth.

FOR THE SOUP

2 tablespoons extra virgin olive oil

2 medium yellow onions, sliced

2 pounds shelling beans, shelled (substitute 1 cup dried beans, such as cannellini beans, navy beans, or Great Northern beans, picked through, rinsed, soaked overnight in 3 cups cold water, and drained)

½ pound fresh green beans, trimmed (substitute frozen — no need to thaw them — but not canned)

4 small carrots, sliced

2 small (or 1 medium) red-skinned or new potatoes, peeled and diced

1 medium zucchini, diced

2 small leeks (or 4 scallions), both green and white parts, sliced and well rinsed

4 ripe tomatoes (substitute a 14-ounce can whole tomatoes, drained), cored and diced

2 bay leaves

6 fresh thyme sprigs or 2 teaspoons dried thyme

½ teaspoon fine sea salt

¼ teaspoon freshly ground pepper

⅔ cup elbow macaroni

FOR THE PISTOU

4 garlic cloves

2 cups (packed) fresh basil leaves

½ cup freshly grated Gruyère, about 1½ ounces (substitute Parmesan)

¼ to ⅓ cup extra virgin olive oil

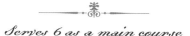

Serves 6 as a main course

SOUPE DE POULET GRATINÉE AUX BAIES ROSES

Gratinéed Chicken Soup with Pink Peppercorns

*W*hen winter comes around and multiple layers of woolen cardigans become permanently affixed to my body, my anti-chill strategy is to cook up gallon upon gallon of hearty soups. This serves the double purpose of warming up the kitchen as the soup simmers, and then myself as I gulp down the mixture, my hands cupped around the steaming bowl.

On those days, I am particularly drawn to soups that are a self-contained meal, and this one is exactly that: a rich soup of chicken and onions, jazzed up by pink peppercorns. Topped with bread and grated cheese, each bowl is gratinéed under the broiler, in French onion soup fashion. The underbelly of the bread absorbs the broth while the crust remains crisp, and the softened surface, covered with bubbly cheese, welcomes the spoon that will tear it apart.

It is a rustic and invigorating dish that I serve in the shallow earthenware bowls that Maxence's grandparents gave us when they had to sell their beloved country house. Not only have these bowls witnessed many a grandchild's slurp, but they also have little ears that make them easy to handle when I take them out of the oven in my mismatched oven mitts. The soup can be cooked and served on the same day, but make it ahead if you can: the flavors will deepen overnight.

PINK PEPPERCORNS *In the colorful family of peppercorns, the pink peppercorn is the adopted child: it is a berry just like its black, white, and green siblings, but it grows on an unrelated plant called Baies Rose, cultivated in South America and on the islands of La Réunion and Madagascar in the Indian Ocean. Pink peppercorns are delicately peppery, with fruity and floral notes. You can buy them dried from specialty foods stores and spice specialists. They go well with poultry, fish, and eggs; you can use them in spice rubs, sauces, and dressings, or to add zing to sweet recipes — chocolate desserts, berry salads, and crunchy cookies, such as biscotti or navettes (see page 222).* ❦

1. Set a large soup pot over medium-high heat. Add the chicken thighs, skin side down, and season with salt. Cook for 3 to 4 minutes on each side, until golden, stirring them around a little so the meat won't stick to the bottom. (Be careful not to burn yourself with the sizzling chicken fat.)

2. Remove the chicken from the pot and set aside on a plate. Pour out and discard the excess fat from the pot. Lower the heat to medium-low. Melt the butter in the pot, add the garlic and onions, season with salt, and stir. Cover and cook for 25 minutes, stirring from time to time to avoid coloring, until the onions are very soft.

3. While the onions are cooking, remove the skin from the chicken thighs — don't worry if you can't remove all of it. When the onions are soft, add the flour, if using, and stir to blend. Add the chicken, bay leaves, wine, and stock. Grind the peppercorns with a mortar and pestle or spice grinder, or by crushing them on a cutting board with a rolling pin. Reserve 1 teaspoon for garnish, and add the rest to the pot. Bring the soup to a simmer, cover, and cook for 30 to 35 minutes, until the chicken is cooked through. Let it simmer for 20 more minutes, uncovered. (The recipe can be made a day ahead up to this point. Let cool, cover, and refrigerate. The next day, skim the chicken fat from the surface.)

FOR THE SOUP

2 pounds free-range chicken thighs, with skin and bones

Fine sea salt

1 tablespoon unsalted butter

2 garlic cloves, green sprout removed if any, finely minced

2 pounds yellow onions, thinly sliced

1 tablespoon all-purpose flour to thicken the broth (optional)

2 bay leaves

1/2 cup dry white wine

6 cups vegetable or chicken stock, preferably homemade

2 tablespoons dried pink peppercorns (substitute 1 tablespoon mixed dried peppercorns, from a mix that includes white and pink peppercorns)

FOR THE GRATINÉED TOPPING

Four to six 1/2-inch-thick medium slices day-old peasant-style bread, about 1 1/2 ounces each (if the bread is fresh, dry the slices for 5 to 10 minutes in a 200°F oven)

4 to 6 ounces freshly grated Comté or Gruyère

Serves 4 to 6 as a main course

4. Preheat the oven on the broiler setting. Remove the chicken thighs from the pot and bone them with a fork and knife. Discard the bones and any remaining strips of skin, and cut the meat into bite-size chunks. Return the meat to the pot, stir, taste the broth, and adjust the seasoning. Ladle the soup into ovenproof bowls or soup plates, top each with a slice of bread, and sprinkle with grated cheese.

5. Put the bowls under the broiler for a few minutes, watching them closely, until the cheese is melted, bubbly in places, and lightly golden. (If your oven isn't large enough to accommodate all the bowls, work in batches: the first bowls will be a bit less hot than the last, but still hot enough.) Sprinkle with the reserved peppercorns and serve: set each bowl on a folded napkin if your table needs to be protected from heat, and warn your guests that the bowls and soup will be very hot.

*W*INE DR. KONSTANTIN FRANK DRY RIESLING 2005 (USA, New York, white) Lightly sweet and food-friendly, this wine offers a good balance that plays off the caramelized onions and the spice from the pink peppercorns.

VELOUTÉ DE CHÂTAIGNE & CHAMPIGNONS

Chestnut and Mushroom Soup

I have a thing for chestnuts. Sucking rapturously on a tube of sweet chestnut paste, buying a paper cone of roasted chestnuts from a sidewalk stand and burning the tips of my fingers as I pry their shells open, gobbling up a glazed chestnut and licking its sticky wrapper: these are some of the things chestnuts will make me do — sometimes in public, too.

Their autumnal personality, sweet and earthy and toasty, makes them perfect for comforting, luxurious soups; this one combines roasted chestnuts with fresh mushrooms for a little forest reunion. Since chestnuts are a little pricey and take some effort to roast and peel, this soup is best suited to evenings when you have time and feel like treating yourself, or when you have company.

1. Heat the olive oil in a large soup pot over medium heat. Add the shallots, garlic, and leek. Cook for 5 minutes, stirring regularly, until softened. Deglaze with brandy, if using, or 3 tablespoons warm water (pour in the liquor or water and scrape the bottom of the pot with a wooden spoon).

2. If you are using vacuum-packed or jarred chestnuts, pat them dry with paper towels. Add the chestnuts to the pot and cook for 4 minutes, stirring gently from time to time, until the chestnuts are lightly golden.

3. Reserve two mushrooms for garnish. Slice the remaining mushrooms and add them to the pot. Add the chile powder if desired. Pour in the stock and season with salt. Bring to a simmer, cover, lower the heat to medium-low, and cook for 20 to 30 minutes, until the vegetables are soft.

4. Let the soup cool for a few minutes. Purée the soup using an immersion blender, until the soup is smooth with just a few remaining chunks. Stir in the balsamic vinegar, taste, and adjust the seasoning. (The soup can be made a day ahead up to this point.) Reheat and ladle into bowls. Cut the reserved mushrooms in slices, and chop the parsley leaves roughly. Plop a mushroom slice on the surface of each bowl, sprinkle with parsley and a touch of freshly ground pepper, and serve.

*W*INE BRANCOTT VINEYARDS 2004 PINOT NOIR MARLBOROUGH (New Zealand, Marlborough, red) The typical Pinot Noir flavors of black fruit are joined by a light earthiness that complements the mushrooms, while the dusty cocoa and toasty-spicy oak notes respond to the chestnuts. It is fruity and light, with a gentle acidity and low tannins.

1 tablespoon extra virgin olive oil

2 small shallots, sliced

1 garlic clove, minced

1 leek, white part only, trimmed, cut in $1/2$-inch slices, and rinsed thoroughly

3 tablespoons brandy, such as Armagnac or Cognac (optional)

1 pound fresh chestnuts, roasted and peeled (see page 55; substitute 15 ounces peeled and cooked vacuum-packed or jarred chestnuts)

1 pound cremini mushrooms, brushed clean, stems cut off

A pinch of ground chile powder (optional)

6 cups vegetable stock, preferably homemade

Fine sea salt

2 tablespoons balsamic vinegar

Fresh flat-leaf parsley leaves for garnish

Freshly ground pepper

———— ❋ ————

*Serves 4 as a main course,
6 as a starter*

Velouté de Châtaigne & Champignons
Chestnut and Mushroom Soup, page 52

Roasting Chestnuts Freshly roasted chestnuts give this soup its distinctive flavor and nubby texture. Fresh chestnuts are available at green-markets and some grocery stores between October and December, or they can be ordered online. Start with 1 pound fresh, unshelled chestnuts, shiny and heavy for their size. Carve an X on the rounded side of each nut with a sharp knife. Spread on a baking sheet, and place a heatproof cup filled with water on the baking sheet to prevent the chestnuts from drying. Roast for 20 to 30 minutes in a 400°F oven, until the shells crack open and the flesh inside is tender when tested with the tip of a knife. Let stand until cool enough to handle but still warm and peel the shell and pithy skin around the nuts. Discard those that appear to be moldy. (The chestnuts can be roasted up to a day in advance.)

For a speedier preparation, and although the flavor won't be quite as deep, buy peeled and cooked chestnuts at a specialty foods store. Choose chestnuts that are vacuum-packed or jarred; broken pieces are cheaper than whole, and they work fine in soups. Avoid canned, as they are often watery and bland.

SOUPE GLACÉE AUX POUSSES D'ÉPINARD & CREVETTES

Baby Spinach and Shrimp Chilled Soup

*O*n warm summer nights, when the heat of the day is just starting to subside and it seems like the sun might never set, there is nothing like a chilled soup to refresh and sate you — especially if you serve it in a tall glass, like a nutritious savory shake, to accentuate its quenching powers.

This one offers a surprising mix of nutty, green, and marine flavors. It will serve as a wonderfully light main dish if your appetite has melted in the heat, or a refreshing start to an alfresco meal in the cool backyard — I don't have a backyard, but I just sit by the open window and pretend. Serve with toasted fingers of crusty bread, to dip and soak and munch as you drink.

2 tablespoons extra virgin olive oil

2 garlic cloves, finely minced

6 tablespoons pine nuts

8 cups (packed) baby spinach leaves, about 8 ounces

2 cups good-quality cooked and shelled baby shrimp, about 8 ounces — fresh or frozen, thawed, and drained

2 cups plain kefir — a thin drinkable yogurt, available from natural foods stores, Middle Eastern markets, and some grocery stores (substitute buttermilk)

Fine sea salt and freshly ground pepper

1 tablespoon to $^1/_4$ cup milk

※

Serves 4 as a main course, 6 as a starter
Chilling time: 1 hour

1. Heat the olive oil in a large skillet over medium heat. Add the garlic and pine nuts and cook for 3 minutes, stirring regularly, until golden and fragrant. Add the spinach and shrimp and cook for a minute, until the spinach is just wilted. Transfer onto a plate and let cool for a few minutes.

2. Combine the spinach mixture and kefir in a medium mixing bowl if you are using an immersion blender, or in a food processor. Sprinkle with salt and pepper and process until smooth. If the mixture is a little thick, add a little milk, a tablespoon at a time, until it reaches the desired consistency. Cover and chill for an hour, or up to a day. Stir, taste, and adjust the seasoning. Pour into glasses and serve with toasted fingers of crusty bread, and Tabasco or lemon juice on the side, if desired.

Soupe Glacée aux Pousses d'Épinard & Crevettes
Baby Spinach and Shrimp Chilled Soup

VARIATION Instead of using cooked baby shrimp, cook 1 pound fresh jumbo shrimp in a skillet with a little olive oil and garlic. Set four to six of them aside for garnish, depending on the number of servings you want to make. Shell and devein the rest of the shrimp, and process them with the spinach and kefir as instructed. Serve in glasses, with one reserved shrimp on the rim of each glass.

Œufs

EGGS

Œuf à la Coque, Mouillettes à l'Artichaut
SOFT-BOILED EGG WITH ARTICHOKE BREAD FINGERS

Piperade

Œuf Cocotte

Frittata Fève & Menthe
FAVA BEAN AND MINT FRITTATA

ŒUF À LA COQUE, MOUILLETTES À l'ARTICHAUT

Soft-boiled Egg with Artichoke Bread Fingers

Œuf à la coque — literally, egg in the shell — was the ritual Sunday night dinner at my parents' house. Each member of the family had his personal eggcup: mine was ceramic, with a tacky little goose attached to the side, wearing a blue polka dot bonnet and nothing else. On Sunday nights my mood was often melancholy — the weekend fun was over and there was school, perhaps a chemistry test, in the morning — but the goose and the œuf à la coque usually lifted my spirits. As soon as my mother brought in the steaming eggs, freshly lifted from the pan of boiling water, we would all get busy popping their hats open and buttering our *mouillettes*.

Mouillettes (moo-yet) are slim fingers of toasted bread, a small set of edible cutlery with which to stir and scoop out the insides of the egg. They are typically spread with butter (optionally sprinkled with fleur de sel), but I like to dress mine with whatever apparel strikes my fancy. In this recipe, the bread is coated with a smooth spread of artichoke and goat cheese: it can be prepared as the eggs cook, and its subtle sweetness is a beautiful complement to the runny yolk.

I recommend the œuf à la coque when you aspire to a blissfully simple supper — whether you need cheering up or not — and it fares well for brunch, too. Since the egg is the lead actor here, use the best quality you can find: I buy mine from the greenmarket or the cheese shop, where the farm-fresh eggs boast a rich, almost buttery flavor, and where one scores extra points for bringing one's own empty egg box.

HOW TO EAT AN ŒUF À LA COQUE *Tap the egg gently with a knife all around the pointy top, and slice off the "hat" you have thus loosened. Sprinkle salt and pepper on the inside of the hat and into the egg. Scoop out the inside of the hat with a spoon and eat that first. Take one mouillette, dip it in the egg, and eat the yolk-coated end. Repeat until all the bread has been consumed. Go back to your good old spoon, and scoop out the bits of egg white that remain. Enjoy the unique sound and sensation of the spoon scraping against the shell. Lick your lips, and drop the hat into the empty eggshell for good luck.* ❧

1. Fill a medium saucepan with enough hot water to cover the eggs. Bring the water (without the eggs) to a gentle boil. Lower the eggs cautiously into the water with a slotted spoon. When the water boils again, lower the heat so the water is just simmering, and cook for 4 minutes.

2. While the eggs are cooking, purée the artichokes and goat cheese in a food processor until smooth. (This can also be used as a spread or dip for a quick appetizer; it will keep for a few days.)

3. Slice the baguette horizontally as you would for a sandwich. Toast it and spread with the artichoke mixture. Cut into fingers, thin enough to be easily inserted into the egg. Sprinkle with thyme and pepper.

4. Drain the eggs and sit them snugly in eggcups (shot or cordial glasses work well, too). Serve with the bread fingers and follow the eating instructions on page 60.

4 extra-fresh high-quality large eggs, at room temperature (or the shells may crack as you lower the eggs into the simmering water)

One 6-ounce jar marinated artichoke hearts, well drained

$^1/_4$ cup fresh goat cheese

About 4 ounces fresh baguette (or thick slices of peasant-style bread)

Fresh or dried thyme

Freshly ground pepper

Serves 4 as a light main course

PIPERADE

*M*y first encounter with *piperade* (peep-a-rad) was at my friend Laurence's apartment one night. When I arrived, sweet smells of stewed peppers and tomatoes met me at the door, seeping from the kitchen. The rest of our friends were nursing pre-dinner drinks in the living room; I joined Laurence by the stove to offer a hand.

"There's not much to do," she said, lifting the lid of the pan to show me, "just a bit of stirring and waiting." This gave me the opportunity to snoop around her kitchen cabinets as we shared breaking news from our lives. When the vegetables had softened and the juices had reduced, she poured in more eggs than I had ever seen used at

Œuf à la Coque, Mouillettes à l'Artichaut
Soft-Boiled Egg with Artichoke Bread Fingers, page 60

Œuf Cocotte, page 65

once — there were eight of us to feed, many of them young men with large appetites — stirred them around until just set, and called everyone to the table.

At the first forkful, I was smitten. Piperade may look to the untrained eye like a simple omelet, but it is more than the sum of its parts. As the vegetables slowly simmer, their flavors concentrate and deepen to a sweet richness, and at that point they are just begging for the pillowy embrace of the eggs.

Piperade is a specialty from the French Basque country, and the original recipe calls for a good pinch of *piment d'Espelette* (a red chile pepper, hand-harvested and wreathed into garlands to dry out on house façades), but any kind of moderately hot chile powder may be used. It is traditionally served as a first course, but following Laurence's example I prefer it as a main dish for a simple summer dinner, with thin slices of dry-cured ham on the side to exalt the piperade's sweetness. In keeping with the regional theme I use ham from Bayonne; prosciutto, Parma, or Serrano ham will be just as good.

1 tablespoon extra virgin olive oil

2 medium yellow onions, sliced

2 garlic cloves, minced

2 medium bell peppers, one green, one yellow, cut in strips

A pinch of ground chile powder

4 medium tomatoes

Fine sea salt

$1/2$ teaspoon sugar (optional)

8 extra-fresh high-quality large eggs

Serves 4 as a main course, 6 to 8 as a starter (the recipe can be doubled in a very large sauté pan)

1. Heat the olive oil in a large sauté pan. Add the onions, garlic, bell peppers, and ground chile powder. Cover and cook over medium-low heat for about 45 minutes, until very soft, stirring from time to time. If the vegetables start to stick to the pan, add a tablespoon of water.

2. In the meantime, blanch and peel the tomatoes: fill a medium saucepan with enough water to cover them and bring to a simmer (without the tomatoes). Remove from heat and lower the tomatoes into the water with a slotted spoon. Let sit for a minute and remove with the spoon. Let cool and then peel, core, and quarter the tomatoes. Discard the juices and seeds.

3. When the peppers and onions are very soft, add the tomatoes, season with salt and sugar, if using, and cook uncovered over medium heat for 20 minutes, until all the moisture has evaporated. (The vegetables can be cooked up to a day ahead and refrigerated in an airtight container.)

4. Crack the eggs in a medium mixing bowl, season with salt, and beat very lightly with a fork, just to break the yolks. Pour into the pan and cook over medium-high heat for a few minutes, stirring gently with a spatula, until soft curds form and the eggs are almost set, but still a little runny. Serve immediately — transfer into a warmed dish or serve straight from the pan — with thinly sliced dry-cured ham, if desired.

*W*INE MIONETTO IL N/V PROSECCO (Italy, Veneto, sparkling white) Although this sparkler is a dry wine, the fruit flavors of apple and pear are almost sweet and play nicely with the caramelized vegetables. Light-bodied with a clean finish, it dances around your palate with a citrusy, bubbly acidity.

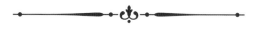

ŒUF COCOTTE

*W*hen I was nine and in the last year of primary school, I didn't have class on Wednesdays. And since my parents considered me old enough to be home without a sitter, I was responsible for my own lunch. My memory may fail me, but I seem to remember that this involved a lot of canned ravioli, warmed up in a saucepan.

It is around that time that my parents got our first microwave oven, for which I developed an odd fascination. I remember my amazement when we brought the first cup of water to a boil, the solemn warning about not running it empty and not putting anything metal in it, the panicky fright when I accidentally did (it could have been a can of ravioli) and miniature fireworks ensued.

This microwave oven came with a recipe booklet. I knew nothing about cooking then, but I read the book carefully and spotted the one thing that seemed doable: a recipe for *œuf cocotte*, which soon joined the beef ravioli in the Wednesday lunch rotation.

Œuf cocotte is simply an egg cooked in a ramekin over other ingredients (usually ham and cream), with an optional topping of grated cheese. This was, in effect, the first recipe I ever followed, the first dish I ever made from scratch and unsupervised. Of course, eggs cooked in the microwave were impossibly rubbery — they even imploded if you left them in for too long — but the pride of eating a dish I had prepared myself was compensation enough.

Now that I am older and can be trusted to use a conventional oven without putting my life in any immediate danger, I make œuf cocotte the traditional way, baked in the oven. It is an easy and adaptable recipe, equally suited to lunch, dinner, or brunch. It is also well received as a first course for a casual dinner party.

1 pat unsalted butter for greasing ramekins

2 tablespoons crème fraîche, or sour cream

1 ounce thinly sliced dry-cured ham, shredded in $1/2$-inch strips (I use jambon de Bayonne or jambon d'Ardèche, but prosciutto, Parma, or Serrano ham will be fine, too)

2 extra-fresh high-quality large eggs

6 cherry tomatoes, halved

Fine sea salt and freshly ground pepper

1 tablespoon snipped fresh chives

❋

Serves 2 as a light main course (the recipe can be doubled or tripled)

1. Preheat the oven to 400°F and grease two 6-ounce ramekins with butter. Drop a spoonful of cream in each ramekin and top with the ham. Break one egg into each ramekin without rupturing the yolks, top with the tomatoes, and season with salt and pepper.

2. Place the ramekins in a baking dish large enough to accommodate them and pour hot water in the dish halfway up the ramekins (this helps conduct the heat gently and evenly around them). Place the dish in the oven and bake for 15 to 18 minutes, depending on how runny you like your eggs.

3. Remove the dish from the oven and the ramekins from the dish (the ramekins will be hot). Sprinkle with chives and serve immediately, with crusty bread for dipping.

VARIATIONS Apart from the egg and cream, all the ingredients can be changed based on what you have on hand: cooked bacon, chicken, or smoked tofu; mushrooms (fresh, or dried and rehydrated), leeks, or zucchini; and any herb or spice you like. You can add a spoonful of onion confit, a sliver of foie gras, or a bit of cheese (grated Comté, shavings of Parmesan, diced goat cheese).

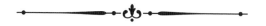

FRITTATA FÈVE & MENTHE

Fava Bean and Mint Frittata

*F*ava beans come in large fat pods that look a lot like giant green beans. The beans hang on to the inside of the cotton-lined pod like métro riders clutching the overhead handrail, in this case a thin membrane that is easily detached. Oval with a slight depression on one side, fava beans are a pretty pistachio green, with a darker spot in the middle.

Now, I am going to be very frank about this, fava beans like to play hard-to-get: after opening each pod, you have to pluck the beans by running your thumb inside. Alas, once they are shelled, you're only halfway there: unless you are dealing with very small and very young beans, the tasty part is still hiding under a layer of waxy skin that should be peeled, to reveal the brighter green morsel inside.

This is a bit of work, but I hope you won't get discouraged: the beans can be prepared a day or two in advance, and their taste and texture will make it worth your while. As the beans pop between your teeth like meaty nuts, they will reveal their sweet, grassy flavor. If you don't feel up to the task, however, use frozen fava beans: I promise not to report you to the authorities.

FAVA BEAN ALLERGY *Be wary of fava beans if you or your dining companions are of Mediterranean, African, or Southeast Asian descent: a portion of the population from these areas, mostly men, suffer from a genetic disorder that makes them seriously allergic to them.* 🌱

This frittata celebrates the fleeting appearance of fava beans in early spring. Once the beans are ready it is quick to assemble, and it will bake while you go do something important, like polish your toenails in preparation for the strappy-sandal-wearing days. It is a sort of oven-baked omelet, lightly fluffy and clean-flavored. Equally tasty warm or at room temperature, it can be cut in slices and served as a main dish for a simple dinner or as a starter. The leftovers may be turned into a portable lunch to bring to the office and make your coworkers fava-green with envy.

3 cups vegetable or chicken stock, preferably homemade, or water

1 1/2 pounds unshelled fresh fava beans, shelled (substitute 1 1/3 cups frozen shelled fava beans or frozen peas — no need to thaw them)

1 teaspoon olive oil for greasing pan

6 extra-fresh high-quality large eggs

1/3 cup light cream

1 cup coarsely grated hard sheep's milk cheese, about 3 1/2 ounces (I use Ossau-Iraty, but Manchego, Pecorino Romano, or crumbled feta will work well, too)

12 fresh mint leaves, chopped

1/4 teaspoon salt

Freshly grated nutmeg (use a whole nutmeg and a fine grater)

Freshly ground pepper

Serves 4 as a main course, 6 to 8 as a starter

1. Unless your fava beans are small and young, their waxy skin needs to be removed. To do this, bring the stock to a boil in a medium saucepan. Drop in the shelled beans and cook for 5 minutes (6 if the beans are frozen). Drain and drop into a bowl of ice-cold water to stop the cooking. Cut a tiny slit in the outer skin of each bean with your thumbnail, and pinch the skin to slip it off — you will get more dexterous as you go. (The beans can be prepared up to 2 days in advance and refrigerated in an airtight container.)

2. Preheat the oven to 425°F. Grease a 9-inch round cake pan with olive oil and line the bottom with parchment paper.

3. In a large mixing bowl, whisk together the eggs, cream, cheese, and mint. Season with salt, a few gratings of nutmeg, and a few turns of the pepper mill. Add the beans, stir gently to combine, and pour into the prepared cake pan.

4. Put into the oven to bake for 25 minutes, until golden and puffy. Transfer the pan on a rack to cool for 5 minutes — the top will settle. Remove from the pan and serve, warm or at room temperature, with a salad of mixed greens. This will keep for up to a day, tightly wrapped and refrigerated.

*W*INE NIGL 2004 KREMSER FREIHEIT GRÜNER VELTLINER (Austria, Lower Austria, white) The nose of this wine is herbal, floral, and slightly spicy, with hints of white pepper. Light-bodied and fresh with a moderate acidity, it offers flavors of mint and Thai basil, the tartness of underripe plums, and the salty minerality of — yes — wet stones.

Frittata Fève & Menthe
Fava Bean and Mint Frittata

Invitation

ENTERTAINING

While I love eating out with friends, having them at home is something else entirely: the atmosphere is more intimate, you get to choose your own musical ambiance, and you're free to partake in the kind of conversation you wouldn't dream of letting anyone overhear in a crowded bistro. Of course, that means no eavesdropping for you, either, but you can't win on all counts.

Whether you are inviting friends for a simple apéritif, putting together an impromptu dinner, planning a more elaborate menu, or throwing a party, this section offers tips and recipes to make the occasion stress-free and successful.

Apéro

APÉRITIF

Mousse de Thon à la Pomme Verte
TUNA AND GREEN APPLE MOUSSE

Caviar d'Aubergine
EGGPLANT CAVIAR

Tapenade aux Deux Olives
TWO-OLIVE TAPENADE

Pesto de Pistache
PISTACHIO PESTO

Madeleines au Roquefort, Poire & Noix
WALNUT, PEAR, AND ROQUEFORT MADELEINES

Gougères au Cumin
CUMIN CHEESE PUFFS

Allumettes Noisette Thym
HAZELNUT THYME MATCHSTICKS

$\mathcal{S}$haring an apéritif with friends is one of the customs that earned the French their reputation as a people who take the time to slow down, unwind, and enjoy the finer things in life — well, food and drink, mostly.

While this pre-dinner drink is often enjoyed at a café, having guests over for the apéritif is also very common. It is an informal way to entertain, requiring less work and forethought than a full-blown dinner party. This pressure-free invitation is often the first that is extended to people one doesn't know very well — neighbors who have just moved in, coworkers, or new acquaintances. It is just as popular among old friends, with whom an *apéro* may be improvised at the last minute.

Everyone gathers around the coffee table in early evening and chats over drinks and a few nibbles. After an hour or two the guests will leave, or the whole party will go out for dinner. A slight variation is the *apéro dînatoire* (dining apéritif), for which the host prepares enough appetizers to satisfy everyone's hunger: the evening will fly by in lively conversation, and there will be no talk of further dinner plans. I am very fond of the casual atmosphere of such occasions: people feel relaxed and comfortable; they can come and go as they please and mingle to their heart's content without being limited to one end of the table.

Apéritif food is by essence very simple, and the only real rule is that one should be able to eat without plates or silverware. At a café or wine bar you might order a charcuterie plate — bite-size pieces of bread topped with *saucisson* or some kind of pâté. If the apéro is hosted at home, there are many ways to put food on the coffee table with little shopping or preparation. The deli will provide me with marinated vegetables, olives, or anchovies, and I will buy a slice of game terrine or strips of dry-cured ham from the charcuterie. We always have cheese in the fridge (I stick to mild ones for the apéritif), and I'll drop by the bakery for a fresh baguette.

The exercise is even easier if there is bread in the freezer and a few well-chosen canned or jarred items in the pantry. I like to buy local specialties when I travel and give my guests a taste of the region I was visiting. From the French Basque country I might bring back *boudin basque* and roasted *piquillos*. From the Périgord, foie gras, onion confit, and duck *rillettes*. From Brittany, quality sardines, fish pâtés, and pickled salicornia. From Alsace, a spread of snails and garlic and a Gewürztraminer jelly to pair with foie gras. But since I like to play in the kitchen and cook for my friends (read: test recipes on them), I mix and match these ready-to-serve items with a few homemade ones.

Apéritif Drinks A wide range of drinks can be served for the apéritif, provided they're refreshing and not too strong — the idea is to open the appetite, not dull the brain. A light-bodied wine (red or white), a chilled Muscat (a sweet wine), a port, or an apéritif liqueur such as Martini, Pineau des Charentes, Pastis, or Lillet. Simple, not-too-cloying cocktails are also welcome, especially kir, a mix of crème de cassis (black currant liqueur) and white wine from Burgundy. And Champagne is a must if you feel in a celebratory mood (a kir royal mixes Champagne with crème de cassis). Ideally, you should offer a choice of drinks from your liquor cabinet — bonus points if it is hidden behind a collapsible bookshelf. Finally, make sure you have sparkling water and fruit or tomato juice, for those who prefer a nonalcoholic beverage.

MOUSSE DE THON À LA POMME VERTE

Tuna and Green Apple Mousse

$\mathcal{D}$ips and spreads are ideal for an apéritif: most are easy to prepare, and their do-it-yourself approach invites guests to dunk and daub and scoop and smear, which they love to do — just keep a few napkins close by. I serve them with bite-size pieces of crusty bread and assorted crudités: cherry tomatoes and cucumber sticks, but also pink radishes, crisp leaves of baby lettuce, sticks of raw zucchini or fennel, apple slices . . . I spread a few slices of bread in advance and arrange them on a plate — this encourages people to start digging in — but once that's devoured I just place a spoon in the bowl and let everyone help himself.

This refreshing and lightly spicy tuna mousse calls for ingredients that most cooks will have on hand, and it is a breeze to put together: you just whiz everything into a smooth and creamy mixture, ready to be thickly spread or dipped into.

Combine all the ingredients in a food processor and process until smooth. Taste and adjust the seasoning. (Alternatively, finely chop the ingredients and combine with a fork.) Transfer to an airtight container and refrigerate for 30 minutes, or up to a day. Stir, and serve with rye crackers, thin slices of baguette, or vegetable sticks.

One 6-ounce can good-quality tuna packed in olive oil, drained

1 small shallot, quartered

$1/2$ crisp green apple, cored and quartered

2 tablespoons freshly squeezed lime juice

$1/4$ cup (lightly packed) fresh cilantro leaves

$1/4$ cup fresh cheese, such as ricotta, fresh goat cheese, or cream cheese

$1/4$ to $1/2$ teaspoon ground chile powder

$1/4$ teaspoon fine sea salt

$1/4$ teaspoon freshly ground pepper

Makes 1 cup
Chilling time: 30 minutes

CAVIAR D'AUBERGINE

Eggplant Caviar

When Maxence and I moved into our Paris apartment, we were still quite unaware of the bonus gift that life had thrown into the bargain: right next door lived a couple just a bit older than us, with whom we were to become excellent friends.

We first met on the night of our housewarming party: we had posted a note in the hall, apologizing for the soon-to-come ruckus, and inviting anyone who so desired to join us for a drink. Quite a few of our new neighbors dropped by — a very favorable omen — and among them, Stephan and Patricia. After that party there was an invitation for an apéritif, which led to another one for dinner, and another one for coffee. Soon enough we were inseparable, chatting from window to window, plucking from each other's herb gardens, borrowing books, sharing a wireless Internet connection, and generally having a grand time.

The secret to an outstanding eggplant caviar lies in the eggplants you use: choose firm and shiny specimens, the smaller the better. Sweeter and thinner-skinned than large ones, small eggplants have fewer seeds, too, which means no bitter aftertaste.

But what binds us most strongly is probably our shared love of food: Patricia is an enthusiastic eater and Stephan a talented home chef, with a real knack for improvisation. I often cook to the clattering sound track of his pots and pans across the wall, many a tasting sample has been swapped between our kitchens, and being invited to dinner next door always holds the promise of a homemade feast.

Among Stephan's much acclaimed specialties is his roasted eggplant caviar. I am normally hopeless at cooking eggplant (bitter and chewy sponges, anyone?), but this caviar I really wanted to replicate. Stephan gladly shared the recipe — or rather the overall process, for he is a no-recipe kind of guy — and to my delighted surprise, it worked like a charm. Eggplant caviar has a rich, velvety texture, yet it is very refreshing, and this makes it welcome in the summer and early fall, when eggplants are at their sweetest. I use it as an appetizer dip or a sandwich spread, or to make the cod mousseline on page 159. It is best made a day ahead.

2 tablespoons extra virgin olive oil, plus
   1 teaspoon for greasing foil

2 pounds eggplants, preferably Italian or
   baby eggplants

2 garlic cloves

2 teaspoons balsamic vinegar

1 teaspoon finely grated lemon zest, from
   an organic lemon

1 tablespoon freshly squeezed lemon juice

$^1/_4$ cup (packed) fresh flat-leaf parsley
   leaves

$^1/_4$ teaspoon whole cumin seeds, toasted

$^1/_2$ teaspoon fine sea salt

Freshly ground pepper

A pinch of ground chile powder

*Makes 2 cups (the recipe
can be halved)
Resting/chilling time:
1 hour for the eggplant,
1 hour for the dip*

1. Preheat the oven to 350°F. Line a baking sheet with foil and grease the foil lightly with oilive oil. Prick the eggplants all over with a fork. Cut a small slit in the most bulbous part of two of the eggplants, and slip a garlic clove into each. Place the eggplants on the baking sheet and bake for an hour, until completely soft, turning the eggplants two or three times during the baking.

2. Remove the baking sheet from the oven. Cut a deep slit down the length of each eggplant, so that it almost (but not quite) reaches the other side. Transfer to a colander, slit side down, and let stand for an hour. (The eggplants can be roasted up to a day ahead and refrigerated in an airtight container lined with paper towels.)

3. Flip the eggplants inside out and shake them gently over the sink to pour out any remaining juices. Scoop out the flesh and garlic and discard the skin and stems. In a food processor, combine the eggplant flesh and garlic with the rest of the ingredients and process until smooth. Taste and adjust the seasoning. Chill for an hour or overnight.

4. Stir, and serve cool with slices of baguette or toasted wedges of pita bread. Eggplant caviar will keep for up to 3 days, covered tightly and refrigerated.

VARIATION Substitute orange zest and 2 tablespoons orange juice for the lemon zest and juice.

TAPENADE AUX DEUX OLIVES

Two-Olive Tapenade

*H*idden in the back of Montmartre is a small restaurant that boasts a cozy patio garden, where you can snatch a table on warm summer nights if you're early or lucky. As soon as you sit on your wobbly chair beneath the trees, the waitress brings a jar of pale green olive paste, homemade and chunky, and thin slices of baguette. It is a simple restaurant, and this initial offering is a much-appreciated gesture: as you study the chalkboard menu and discuss the relative merits of the steak tartare and the braised lamb shank, you can prepare little toasts to fortify your friends and yourself through such crucial dinner decisions.

Homemade tapenade has little to do with store-bought, since freshly crushed olives offer their flavors in much more vivid a way, and I like to serve green and black tapenades side by side, to appreciate their respective traits. They can be made in a food processor, but I prefer the hand-chopped version: it is better suited to spreading than dipping, but this coarse texture makes for fuller flavors.

Using a sharp chef's knife, chop the olives, garlic, anchovies, and capers, setting each ingredient aside separately. In a small bowl, combine the black olives with half the garlic, anchovies, and capers. Add 1 teaspoon of the tomato paste and 1 tablespoon of the olive oil, and mix with a fork to combine. Repeat with the remaining ingredients in a second bowl. Cover and refrigerate for 30 minutes or up to a week. Spread on toasted slices of baguette or crackers.

$2/3$ cup large black olives, such as Kalamata olives, in bulk or from a jar, drained and pitted

$2/3$ cup large green olives, such as Spanish olives (not stuffed), in bulk or from a jar, drained and pitted

1 garlic clove

12 fillets dry-salted anchovies packed in salt or olive oil, drained well and patted dry

$1/4$ cup small capers, drained

2 teaspoons tomato paste

2 tablespoons extra virgin olive oil

Makes $1/2$ cup black tapenade and $1/2$ cup green tapenade
Chilling time: 30 minutes

PESTO DE PISTACHE

Pistachio Pesto

$\mathscr{I}$ don't know of a more underappreciated nut than the pistachio: most people think of it as the stale version that can be found in grocery stores, but the true pistachio, freshly shelled and otherwise unprocessed, has treasures of flavor to reveal. Fashionably green with specks of purple, it has panache and crunch, and its delicate taste makes it a welcome guest in both savory and sweet recipes.

Pistachio pesto is a specialty from Bronte in Sicily, where pistachio trees have been growing since Roman times on the slopes of Mount Etna. A brilliant variation on the classic pesto with pine nuts, pistachio pesto is lushly green and nutty, with an underlying sweetness. This recipe produces a thick paste that can be spread on slices of crusty bread, stuffed in cherry tomatoes for a dainty appetizer, and used in pasta, lasagna, sandwiches, or savory tarts. For a runnier pesto, up the amount of olive oil.

In the bowl of a food processor or mortar, combine the pistachios, garlic, salt, and pepper. Process until coarsely ground. Add the basil, cheese, and $^1/_3$ cup olive oil. Process until smooth, adding a little more oil as needed. Adjust the seasoning. Transfer to a jar, pack with a spoon, and close tightly. Refrigerate for up to a week.

VARIATION Substitute almonds and arugula for pistachios and basil.

If you can only find salted pistachios, rinse them well under cold water in a colander and drain. Spread on a rimmed baking sheet and bake at 350°F for 5 to 7 minutes or until dry, stirring halfway through. Let cool before using. ❧

1 cup good-quality shelled and unsalted pistachios (available from gourmet or natural foods stores, or Middle Eastern markets; if you can only find salted pistachios, see tip above)

2 garlic cloves, chopped

$^1/_2$ teaspoon fine sea salt

$^1/_4$ teaspoon freshly ground pepper

1 cup (packed) fresh basil leaves

$^1/_4$ cup freshly grated Parmesan, about 1 ounce

$^1/_3$ to $^1/_2$ cup olive oil

Makes 1 cup

MADELEINES AU ROQUEFORT, POIRE & NOIX

Walnut, Pear, and Roquefort Madeleines

𝒮here is a lot to be said for the genius of the madeleine shape: beyond its evident loveliness, it offers the perfect proportion of crust to crumb, and a tickling range of textures as you munch your way from one tip to the other. The following recipe is a savory twist on Marcel Proust's beloved treat, in which the pungency of blue cheese holds hands with the sweetness of pears and the rich crunch of walnuts. Serve with a pre-dinner drink in the fall and winter, or atop a salad of greens. If you neither own nor want to invest in madeleine molds, use mini-muffin tins instead.

1. Preheat the oven to 350°F and butter a tray of madeleine molds or mini-muffin tins.

2. Combine the flour and baking powder in a small mixing bowl. In a medium mixing bowl, whisk the eggs, salt, and pepper. Add the oil, buttermilk, and cheese, and whisk again.

3. Sift the flour mixture into the egg mixture and stir with a wooden spoon until incorporated — the batter will be thick. Don't overmix. Fold in the pear and walnuts and stir. (The batter can be prepared up to a day ahead and refrigerated.) Spoon the batter into the molds, filling them by two thirds.

4. Bake for 12 to 16 minutes, until puffy and golden. Transfer to a rack to cool for a few minutes, unmold, and serve warm.

A pat of unsalted butter for the molds

1 1/4 cups all-purpose flour

1 tablespoon baking powder

3 large eggs

1/2 teaspoon fine sea salt

1/2 teaspoon freshly ground pepper

2 tablespoons extra virgin olive oil

1/2 cup buttermilk or plain unsweetened yogurt

3 ounces Roquefort or another kind of blue cheese, crumbled

1 ripe pear, about 8 ounces, peeled, cored, and diced

1/3 cup shelled walnuts, roughly chopped (not too finely)

Makes 24 madeleines

Canapés are the most elemental of appetizers: nothing more, but nothing less, than thin slices of bread, topped with various spreads and ingredients. More a concept than a precise recipe, canapés can be seen as bite-size canvases to play with colors and pairings, using whatever is on hand and in season. For maximum ease of preparation, I assemble them with ingredients that can be used straight from the fridge, jar, or can, and small portions of leftovers that couldn't be recycled into much else. Naturally, since there is no cooking involved, quality is of the essence, both for the toppings and the bread.

The classic French canapé is made on miniature slices of sandwich bread (*pain de mie*), but I find this sorely lacking in texture and taste, and I prefer to use a fresh baguette or a loaf of artisan bread. Specialty breads — with olives, herbs, nuts, and the like — can work well, too, if the toppings match their flavoring. The bread will be thinly sliced, half an inch or less, for an optimal bread-to-topping ratio: the bread is the supporting character here, and should not elbow its way to the front of the stage. Baguettes can be sliced perpendicularly or at a sharp angle, while slices from a loaf should be cut in one- or two-bite pieces. The bread may be rubbed with olive oil or garlic and lightly toasted — not too much, though, or it will be too crisp for its own good. Generally speaking, if the bread is very fresh, I don't tamper with it and just let its supple nature shine.

Canapés

Aside from the flavor complementarity, canapés are most successful when there is a nice textural conversation going on among the ingredients — creamy, smooth, crisp, crunchy, meaty — and when the colors are harmonious. Avoid crowding too many toppings on the same canapé, or some of the flavors will get lost in the battle: two or three is usually a good number. Arrange them on the bread in an appealing and stable way (if the whole thing tumbles down on you as you bring it to your mouth, it is not stable) and serve the canapés lined up on a platter or a wooden cutting board.

Favorite combinations include:

- Fresh goat cheese + thinly sliced prosciutto or other dry-cured ham + fresh figs
- Shavings of sheep's milk cheese (such as Ossau-Iraty or Pecorino Romano) + Spanish chorizo + flat-leaf parsley
- Onion confit + smoked duck breast + chopped walnuts

- Diced tomatoes + marinated anchovies
- Crème fraîche + raw salmon + dill
- Butter + sardines + chervil
- Monkfish liver + thinly sliced scallions + a drop of lemon juice
- Plump snails from Burgundy + a drizzle of *beurre d'escargot* (butter melted with garlic and chopped parsley)
- Fresh cheese + tapenade (see page 79) + arugula
- Goat cheese + toasted pine nuts + a drop of honey
- Pistachio pesto (see page 80) + slow-roasted tomatoes (see page 100)

To figure out how much of each ingredient you should use on your canapés, assemble one, taste it, and adjust the quantities. A strenuous, thankless job, I know, but somebody has to do it.

GOUGÈRES AU CUMIN

Cumin Cheese Puffs

*I*f you ever attend a wine tasting in Burgundy, you will likely be offered a plate of these golden cheese puffs to cleanse your palate and line your stomach between two sips. *Gougères* have a certain air of elegance and old-world sophistication, but they are in fact quite easy to make, and it's a joy to watch them through the oven door, as they puff up and suffuse the kitchen with intoxicating cheese smells. Their thin crust gives way to a soft, pulpy heart, and this texture makes them quite addictive — consider yourself warned.

PÂTE À CHOUX *The basic batter for gougères is called a pâte à choux. Its sweet version (2 tablespoons sugar are added along with the butter) is used in many French pastries, such as* choux à la crème *(cream puffs),* chouquettes *(simple puffs topped with large grains of sugar called* sucre perlé), *chocolate or coffee* éclairs, *or* Paris-Brest, *an over-the-top confection garnished with praline-flavored buttercream.*

The classic version calls for cheese as the only flavoring, but I like to use cumin in mine: this complements the fruitiness of the cheese remarkably well and adds a welcome piquancy. Serve with an apéritif drink, or use the same batter to make large gougères (about 3 inches in diameter) and serve as a first course, with a salad.

1. Measure all the ingredients before you start. Combine the butter, salt, and 1 cup water in a medium saucepan and bring to a simmer over medium-low heat. Remove from heat, add the flour all at once, and stir quickly with a wooden spoon until well blended. Return the pan to medium-low heat and keep stirring until the mixture forms a ball and pulls away from the sides of the pan.

2. Let cool for 3 minutes. Add the eggs one by one, stirring well between each addition, until incorporated. (What you have just made is a *pâte à choux*.) Sprinkle with cumin and pepper and fold in the cheese. The batter will be thick. Cover and refrigerate for 30 minutes, or up to a day.

3. Preheat the oven to 400°F and line a baking sheet with parchment paper. Remove the batter from the fridge, and use two teaspoons to shape small balls of batter (about 1 inch in diameter) that you will plop onto the baking sheet, leaving an inch of space between each. If you have to work in batches, cover the batter and return it to the fridge.

4. Bake for 20 minutes, until puffy and golden — however much you want to peek inside, do not open the oven door during the first 10 minutes of baking, or the gougères will not rise well. Turn off the oven, open the oven door just a crack, and leave the gougères in for another 5 minutes. (This helps prevent an abrupt temperature change, which could cause the gougères to deflate and nobody wants that.) Transfer to a cooling rack for 5 minutes and serve warm, or let cool and serve at room temperature.

NOTE You can freeze the gougères for up to a month and reheat them (no thawing necessary) in a 350°F oven for 8 minutes. They won't be as moist as freshly baked ones, but they are very convenient to have on hand for unexpected guests.

VARIATIONS Replace the cumin with caraway seeds, rosemary, or paprika, or omit the spices altogether.

6 tablespoons unsalted butter, diced

$1/2$ teaspoon fine sea salt

1 cup flour, sifted

4 large eggs

1 teaspoon whole cumin seeds or $1/2$ teaspoon ground cumin

$1/4$ teaspoon freshly ground pepper

$1^1/2$ cups freshly grated Comté or Gruyère, about 5 ounces (substitute a good Swiss cheese)

Makes about 40 gougères
Chilling time: 30 minutes

Gougères au Cumin
Cumin Cheese Puffs, page 84

Allumettes Noisette Thym
Hazelnut Thyme Matchsticks, page 88

ALLUMETTES NOISETTE THYM

Hazelnut Thyme Matchsticks

*O*ver the past few years, Paris has seen new types of food events appear: gallery openings in which the catered buffet matches the exhibition; food and wine tastings in unusual locations (barges, museums, antique butcher shops); renowned chefs cooking on the street or from market stalls and offering their food for free; edible sculptures that disappear into the visitors' stomachs and have to be built afresh the next day . . . These initiatives stem from a desire to look at food in a playful way and are enthusiastically received by the public.

FLEUR DE SEL *Some of the recipes in this book call for fleur de sel, a sea salt that's hand harvested at the surface of salt marshes. It is made of delicate, moist crystals and has a mild, almost flowery flavor. It is not meant for cooking — the crystals would just melt — but rather for the seasoning of a finished dish. It also fares well in baked goods, such as crackers, cookies, and tart crusts. (Kosher salt can be substituted.)*

I've had the opportunity to take part in a few such events, including one in a famous Parisian department store, where my partner Marion Chatelain and I set up a series of tastings that we called Bar à Veloutés (*velouté* means velvety soup). From this bar we served a colorful variety of sweet or savory soups in small shot glasses, with a choice of toppings and dippers, so people could experiment with flavor and texture pairings.

These tastings involve more planning and logistics than one might think, but they are fun and gratifying. You get to see the tasters' reactions up close, and receive instant feedback on your ideas; most visitors are intrigued and appreciative (apart from a few graceless characters, but these are entertaining, too), and the food always disappears in no time, as free food will.

Among the edible stirrers we created for the Bar à Veloutés were these two-bite crackers, thin and crumbly and racy in flavor. I was so taken with them that they were soon added to my repertoire as an oft-prepared and much loved apéritif nibble.

1. In a large mixing bowl, rub the flour and butter together until the mixture forms coarse crumbs. Add the cheese, hazelnuts, thyme, and $1/2$ teaspoon of the salt. Blend well. Add the egg and blend it in with a fork. Once the egg is absorbed, knead the dough lightly until it comes together and forms a ball. It should be smooth enough to be rolled out: if it is too dry, add a little cold water, teaspoon by teaspoon, until it reaches the desired consistency.

2. Divide the dough into two balls, wrap in plastic, and refrigerate for 30 minutes, or up to a day. (If you refrigerate it for more than 2 hours, remove it from the fridge about 15 minutes before you use it, or it will be too hard to work with.)

1 cup all-purpose flour

5 tablespoons chilled unsalted butter

6 tablespoons freshly grated Parmesan, about $1^1/2$ ounces

$3/4$ cup shelled hazelnuts (skin-on for a prettier color effect), very finely chopped

2 teaspoons dried thyme or 4 teaspoons fresh thyme, chopped

1 teaspoon fleur de sel or kosher salt

1 large egg

1 large egg yolk for glazing

Makes about 80 crackers
Chilling time: 30 minutes

3. Preheat the oven to 350°F and line a baking sheet with parchment paper.

4. Remove one ball of dough from the fridge. Roll it out thinly on a well-floured surface to form a rectangle approximately 6 by 8 inches and $1/6$ inch thick. Beat the egg yolk with 1 tablespoon fresh water in a small bowl. Brush this mixture lightly over the rectangle of dough and sprinkle with $1/4$ teaspoon salt.

5. Turn the dough so the longest edge faces you. Use a sharp knife to divide it into vertical strips about $1/4$ inch wide. Cut the rectangle in half horizontally so each strip is 3 inches long. Transfer the strips onto the prepared sheet, leaving $1/2$ inch of space between them. Repeat with the second ball of dough.

6. Bake for 13 to 16 minutes, until golden. Transfer to a rack to cool completely. They will keep for a week in an airtight container at room temperature.

VARIATION For a quicker preparation, shape the dough into two logs (about 1 inch in diameter), put in the freezer for 15 minutes, and slice thinly to form round crackers.

Impromptu

Carpaccio de Courgette au Vinaigre de Framboise
ZUCCHINI CARPACCIO WITH RASPBERRY VINEGAR

Rémoulade de Céleri aux Œufs de Truite
CELERIAC RÉMOULADE WITH TROUT ROE

Papillotes de Bar aux Asperges
ASPARAGUS AND SEA BASS PAPILLOTES

Pain Perdu aux Deux Tomates & Parmesan
TWO TOMATOES AND PARMESAN FRENCH TOAST

Pâtes par Absorption, Courgette & Cacao
CACAO AND ZUCCHINI ABSORPTION PASTA

Poulet Mijoté à la Moutarde
MUSTARD CHICKEN STEW

Tartare au Couteau
HAND-CUT STEAK TARTARE

Boulettes d'Agneau aux Pruneaux
LAMB AND PRUNE MEATBALLS

In dining as in all areas of life, I am very much in favor of spontaneity, improvisation, and drop-of-a-hat decisions. Few things please me more than to talk to a friend in the middle of the afternoon and casually ask, "Well, why don't you come to dinner tonight?" Once plans are made, I have trouble concentrating on anything else as I mentally review the contents of my fridge and dream up a menu that will be quick to shop for and easy to prepare.

Fortunately, I have a few dishes up my sleeve that require just a brief errand for fresh ingredients. Some are no-cook recipes, and some need a little time in the oven or on the stove, but that's time I can spend setting the table or frantically relocating the mess from the living room to the bedroom.

The menu on such occasions is resolutely pared down. We start with an apéritif drink and some quickly assembled canapés (see page 82), and I may skip the first course — no one has ever sued me for this — to focus on the main dish. Dessert will be simple, too: a cup of berries with a little whipped cream, roasted figs and fresh cheese, a warm apple compote with almond *tuiles* from the bakery, or perhaps a good store-bought sorbet.

The key to a successful impromptu dinner is to remember that it's perfectly fine not to have everything ready by the time your guests arrive: everyone realizes you have other responsibilities during the day, and they should appreciate your efforts even if you're still wearing an apron when the doorbell rings. Besides, it looks really cute on you.

CARPACCIO DE COURGETTE AU VINAIGRE DE FRAMBOISE

Zucchini Carpaccio with Raspberry Vinegar

The original carpaccio is a dish of thinly sliced raw beef that was created at Harry's Bar in Venice in 1950. It was named in honor of the fifteenth-century Venetian painter Vittore Carpaccio, who favored red colors in his paintings. The term is now used for various dishes that feature raw and thinly sliced ingredients, red or not, even though this admittedly betrays the etymology.

This carpaccio is a good introduction to the crisp and lightly sweet nature of raw zucchini. It should be made with the freshest zucchini you can find, slender young things with smooth skin and firm flesh. Late spring or summer is the best time to pluck them at the farmer's market, or in your own vegetable garden if you're fortunate enough to have one (in which case I think you should ship me a crate, thanks much).

1. Trim the zucchini and cut it in paper-thin slices, using a sharp knife or a mandoline. Arrange in a circular pattern (starting from the outside and working your way in, each slice overlapping the previous one) on individual plates. Sprinkle the cheese over the slices.

2. Whisk together the vinegar and olive oil in a small bowl and drizzle over the zucchini and cheese. Sprinkle with thyme, salt, and pepper. Cover with plastic wrap and let stand at room temperature for 10 minutes before serving.

VARIATIONS Use balsamic vinegar in place of raspberry vinegar, and shavings of Parmesan or crumbled feta instead of goat cheese. You can also toss the zucchini with the rest of the ingredients in a bowl, and serve it as a salad.

𝒲INE FREIXENET BRUT DE NOIRS, CAVA ROSÉ (Spain, Catalonia, sparkling rosé) This fresh and mouthwatering bubbly wine displays notes of strawberry and raspberry. It is light enough to respect the delicate zucchini flavor, but it has enough tang and acidity to stand up to the vinegar.

3 small zucchini, about 1¼ pounds

3 ounces semidry goat cheese (log-shaped or round), crumbled or cut in shavings

2 tablespoons raspberry vinegar (substitute another kind of fruit vinegar)

¼ cup extra virgin olive oil

1 tablespoon fresh thyme or 1½ teaspoons dried thyme

Fleur de sel or kosher salt

Freshly ground pepper

❉

Serves 6 as a starter

RASPBERRY VINEGAR *is made from fresh raspberries macerated in white wine vinegar for a few months. This tangy and fruity condiment can be found in fine foods stores, and will be a prized addition to your vinegar collection: a few drops will add sparkle to your vinaigrettes, sauces, and marinades, especially for fish and duck.* ❧

Carpaccio de Courgette au Vinaigre de Framboise
Zucchini Carpaccio with Raspberry Vinegar, page 92

Rémoulade de Céleri aux Œufs de Truite
Celeriac Rémoulade with Trout Roe, page 96

RÉMOULADE DE CÉLERI AUX ŒUFS DE TRUITE

Celeriac Rémoulade with Trout Roe

𝒞eleriac is not the most glamorous of vegetables — its unpeeled knobby looks certainly don't help its social life — but once you make its acquaintance you won't be sorry. It can be eaten raw or cooked, and in both cases it offers an elegant flavor profile, sweet and earthy, with notes of cumin and fennel. Although it is the root part of a variety of celery, its taste is only vaguely related to that of the better-known stalk part. So if you don't like celery stalks, don't turn the page quite yet: I don't like them either, but I could eat celeriac every day, for breakfast even.

Céleri rémoulade is a salad of grated celeriac in a creamy herb dressing, and it is up there with the *poireau vinaigrette* (soft leeks served cold with a vinaigrette) and the *œuf mayo* (a hard-boiled egg, split in two and topped with a handsome dollop of mayonnaise) in the classic range of brasserie-style starters. Humble and unassuming, these dishes are frequently botched — especially at office cafeterias — but they are quite delightful when they're executed with just a bit of care.

The traditional rémoulade dressing is made with mayonnaise, yet I prefer this yogurt-based version: it is just as flavorful, but much lighter. In the following dish, céleri rémoulade slips on its best Sunday dress, with frilly fronds of dill and a dollop of trout roe, for a nice color contrast and an enchanting pop-in-your-mouth effect.

1¹/₂ pounds celeriac (about 1 small head, or ¹/₂ medium head)

³/₄ cup plain Greek-style yogurt

2 teaspoons strong Dijon mustard

1 tablespoon freshly squeezed lemon juice

1 garlic clove, pressed or very finely minced

2 tablespoons (packed) dill fronds, plus a few fronds for garnish

Fine sea salt and freshly ground pepper

6 rounded tablespoons trout or salmon roe, about 3¹/₂ ounces — fish roe can be found at fish markets, Asian stores, or specialty foods stores (substitute 4 ounces good smoked salmon, diced)

Serves 6 as a starter
Chilling time: 20 minutes

1. Peel the celeriac, cut it in six sections, and grate them using a box grater or the grater attachment of a food processor — this will yield about 6 cups, loosely packed. (Don't let the grated celeriac stand for too long or it will start to brown.) Combine with the yogurt, mustard, lemon juice, garlic, and dill in a large salad bowl. Season with salt and pepper and mix with a fork to blend. Taste and adjust the seasoning. Cover and refrigerate for at least 20 minutes, an hour if possible, or up to a day.

2. Remove from the fridge, stir, and divide the celeriac mixture among six plates (use cylindrical serving molds if you have them) or transparent glasses. Top with 1 tablespoon roe and garnish with the reserved dill fronds. Serve immediately.

VARIATION The celeriac part of this dish (sans roe) can be served at a picnic or packed for lunch at the office, topped with leftover meat from a roasted chicken.

𝓦INE LUCIEN ALBRECHT CRÉMANT D'ALSACE BRUT BLANC DE BLANCS (France, Alsace, sparkling white) A light and delicate bubbly with refreshing apple flavors and a hint of spice and minerals. The minerality plays off the saltiness of the roe, while the hunger-inducing acidity and bubbles enhance the tangy-creamy rémoulade.

CELERIAC, *also called celery root or knob celery, is in season between October and April. It comes in bulbous, gray-white heads, with knobs and stringy filaments. Choose a small or medium head that feels firm, and knock on it gently to make sure it doesn't sound hollow. If a pixie comes out, apologize and pick another one. Depending on the size of your celeriac, this recipe may leave you with half a head; it will keep for a few days, tightly wrapped and refrigerated. Use it in a soup with sweet potatoes and ginger, braise it in a little white wine, or — and this is my favorite use — boil it, and mash it with a little cream and lots of pepper. We serve this at holiday meals in my family, as a side to a roast goose or boudin blanc, a delicate white sausage sometimes flavored with morels or truffles.* ❧

PAPILLOTES DE BAR AUX ASPERGES

Asparagus and Sea Bass Papillotes

$\mathcal{O}$f all the possible cooking techniques for fish, the *papillote* provides the best effort-to-effect ratio. Behind the pretty French name (pah-pea-yot') is a simple concept: you just wrap a fish fillet and a few choice ingredients in parchment paper and plop the whole thing in the oven. Inside the papillote, a little Turkish bath gets going: the fish cooks gently in its own steam without drying out, and its flavors meld voluptuously with those of the other bathers. It is quick, it is foolproof, and the presentation is fun in a dramatic sort of way: bring the mystery papillotes to the table, snip them open before your guests, and let them take in the aromas that escape from the pouches and dance up to their noses.

WRAPPERS *When I don't want to deal with the folding of parchment paper, I use foil instead, greasing the center of the sheet, closing the foil over the filling, and crimping the sides well. On the other hand, when I'm feeling all crafty, I make origami boxes out of parchment paper (the folding instructions can be found online; type "Japanese box diagram" in your favorite search engine) and cook the fillets in them. The lids of these boxes are not as tight fitting as parchment or foil pouches, but the airtight police haven't found me yet.* ❧

This recipe features sea bass cooked on a bed of asparagus stalks, under a creamy blanket of shallots, orange zest, and toasted almonds. It is a springlike dish that will take kindly to a side of aromatic rice or steamed new potatoes. Keep it for when locally grown asparagus are available: frozen or hothouse specimens are often a cruel disappointment. Sea bass is a lean and firm-textured fish that you can replace with striped bass, mahi-mahi, snapper, or even turbot, if you're feeling opulent.

1. Preheat the oven to 400°F. Have ready a baking sheet and four sheets of parchment paper, about 15 by 15 inches.

2. Pat the fillets dry with paper towels and season with salt and pepper. In a small bowl, combine the shallots and zest and sprinkle with salt and pepper. Cut the aspara-

gus in 2-inch sticks and discard the fibrous butt ends (or use them in a soup). Split the sticks in two lengthwise: this will allow them to cook more quickly.

3. Put one sheet of parchment paper on a work surface in front of you. Fold the sheet in two horizontally and unfold. Line up a quarter of the asparagus sticks side by side an inch below the crease, to form a rectangular shape — make sure you divide the asparagus tips evenly. Sprinkle with salt and pepper and top with one fillet. Spread the fish with 1 tablespoon of the crème fraîche, sprinkle with a fourth of the shallot mixture, and a fourth of the toasted almonds.

4. Fold the top half of the parchment paper down over the fillet so the two edges meet. Make a thin and tight fold all along the joined edges, and repeat until the fold reaches the fillet. Close both open sides of the papillote by folding them into pointy ends and tucking them underneath the package. Transfer onto the baking sheet with a hard spatula. Repeat with the remaining ingredients.

5. Bake for 12 minutes if the fillets are less than an inch thick, 14 minutes for thicker fillets. Transfer the packages cautiously onto serving plates. Scoop rice or potatoes on the side, bring the plates to the table, and snip the papillotes open along the top with scissors or a sharp knife.

VARIATIONS Omit the shallots and zest, and top the cream with sliced strawberries. You can also try cooked leeks and goat cheese, baby spinach and mushrooms, zucchini and tomatoes with tapenade, roasted bell peppers and Spanish chorizo . . . Just keep in mind that the papillotes stay but briefly in the oven; ingredients that require a longer cooking time have to be cooked beforehand.

WINE CROSSROADS WINE COMPANY SAUVIGNON BLANC 2005 (New Zealand, Hawkes Bay, white) Sauvignon Blanc is a good match to simple fish dishes. This one has grassy, herbal qualities, and notes of tangerine that respond to the orange zest.

Four 4-ounce sea bass fillets, boneless and skinless, thawed if frozen

Fine sea salt and freshly ground pepper

$1/4$ cup finely diced shallots, from about 2 small shallots

2 teaspoons (packed) finely grated orange zest, from an organic orange

16 slim green asparagus stalks, about $1^1/4$ pounds

$1/4$ cup crème fraîche or sour cream

$1/4$ cup sliced almonds, toasted until golden (see page 6)

*Serves 4 as a main course
(the recipe can be
halved or doubled)*

PAIN PERDU AUX DEUX TOMATES & PARMESAN

Two Tomatoes and Parmesan French Toast

𝒯he simple act of buying bread always fills me with a deep and primal sense of satisfaction, much like the caveman must have felt when he came back to his darling wife after a hunting expedition, dragging a bloody mammoth leg behind him.

SLOW-ROASTED TOMATOES

Semi-dried, or slow-roasted, tomatoes are fleshier and less salty than sun-dried tomatoes. They can be found at Italian delis and specialty foods stores, or you can make your own. Cut a pound of small ripe tomatoes (Roma, plum, or cherry) in half lengthwise, core them, and discard the juice and seeds. Put the tomatoes on a greased rimmed baking sheet in a single layer, drizzle with olive oil, season with salt and pepper, and toss to coat. Bake for 3 to 4 hours at 200°F, flipping the tomatoes halfway through, until wrinkled but still a little moist. Semi-dried tomatoes will keep for up to 4 days in an airtight container in the fridge, 2 weeks if covered with olive oil. 🌿

Me, I drop by the bakery on my way home, fill my lungs with the freshly baked vapors, and wait in line patiently, admiring the little population of pastries through the glass case, or craning my neck to study the daily bread selection on the tall wooden shelves behind the register.

When it's my turn, I place my order, grapple for the exact change in my purse (the quickest way to win the heart of your *boulangère*), and walk away with my still-warm loaf slipped in a paper bag and tucked under my arm. If it's a baguette, it won't take me more than two and a half steps on the sidewalk to tear off the crusty elbow (*le quignon*) and bite into it with delight — nothing tastes as good as this first mouthful of vibrantly fresh, warm bread.

This ceremony holds the promise of a thick slice with cheese or soup for dinner, a generously buttered tartine for breakfast the next day, and a wholesome sandwich for lunch. Sadly, the magic wanes after a couple of days, and when the bread starts to get a little dry and a little chewy, it is time to make *pain perdu* and give a second life to this "lost bread." The traditional pain perdu is similar to what America calls French toast. This eggy and fluffy dessert-type concoction, meant to use up bread that is past its prime, is served for breakfast or as an after-school snack, lightly sprinkled with sugar. But I don't see any reason to confine the idea to the realm of sweets, and I like to apply it to savory ingredients, too.

The following recipe is a tasty way to recycle leftover peasant-style bread: sliced and egg-dipped, the bread is combined with fresh and dried tomatoes. A bit of grated cheese and a short bake in the oven turn it into a satisfying dish, moist and juicy at the bottom, grilled and crisp at the top. Ideal for a summer night when tomatoes are fragrant and plentiful, it is just as fitting for brunch.

1. Cut the bread in 2-inch-wide pieces. In a large mixing bowl, whisk together the eggs, milk, herbs, $1/4$ teaspoon of the salt, and the pepper. Add the bread, toss to coat, and let stand for 10 minutes, stirring gently every now and then to ensure even coating.

2. In the meantime, core the tomatoes and slice them horizontally in $1/3$-inch slices. Let stand in a colander to drain for 5 minutes. Cut the semi-dried tomato halves in bite-size pieces.

3. Preheat the oven to 400°F and grease a large baking dish with 1 teaspoon olive oil. Arrange the tomato slices over the bottom of the dish, reserving nine of the most attractive for the top. Sprinkle with the remaining $1/4$ teaspoon salt, drizzle with a little olive oil, and top with the garlic and semi-dried tomatoes.

4. Arrange the bread over the tomatoes, pour the remaining egg mixture over the dish, top with the reserved tomato slices, and sprinkle with cheese. (This can be prepared up to 8 hours ahead, covered tightly and refrigerated.)

5. Bake for 20 to 25 minutes, until heated through. Switch to broiler setting and broil for 5 minutes, keep-

10 ounces day-old peasant-style bread, cut in $1/2$-inch-thick slices — if the bread is still fresh, dry the slices for 5 minutes on each side in a 200°F oven

4 large eggs

$1/2$ cup milk

$1 1/2$ teaspoons dried oregano

$1 1/2$ teaspoons herbes de Provence (or a mix of dried rosemary, basil, oregano, and thyme)

$1/2$ teaspoon fine sea salt

$1/4$ teaspoon freshly ground pepper

6 medium Roma tomatoes, about $1 1/2$ pounds

12 semi-dried tomato halves, homemade, vacuum-packed, or packed in oil and drained (see page 100; substitute 12 sun-dried tomato halves packed in oil and drained)

Extra virgin olive oil

2 garlic cloves, finely minced

$1/2$ cup freshly grated Parmesan, about 2 ounces

Serves 4 as a main course

ing an eye on the dish, until the cheese is golden and the bread is crisp at the edges. Serve with a salad of mixed greens.

VARIATION Substitute strips of dry-cured ham for the semi-dried tomatoes.

*W*INE KRIS PINOT GRIGIO DELLE VENEZIE 2004 (Italy, Veneto, white) The pear and apple aromas of this wine are joined by hints of nuts that respond well to the Parmesan. It offers enough crispness to balance the richness of the egg-dipped bread, dry citrusy flavors to accent the tomatoes, and a tart, clean finish.

PÂTES PAR ABSORPTION, COURGETTE & CACAO

Cacao and Zucchini Absorption Pasta

*A*bsorption pasta is a risotto-style technique in which you coat pasta with olive oil, pour just enough stock to cover, and cook until desired tenderness, gradually adding more liquids as necessary. This allows a light coating of starch to develop around the pasta, thickening the sauce and giving each bite a delectable, slippery feel.

The absorption method can be applied to your favorite pasta dishes, as long as you use short pasta — spaghetti or linguine wouldn't be as easy to work with. In the following recipe, the pasta is cooked with slim sticks of zucchini, then topped with aged Parmesan and a sprinkle of cacao nibs (see page 230) for a crunchy, earthy note.

AGED CHEESE *A hunk of extra-aged hard cheese (such as a 36-month-old Parmesan, Comté, or Gouda) is a life-saving item to have on hand: it will keep for months, tightly wrapped and refrigerated, and will work wonders on the simplest of pasta dishes, risotti, and vegetable gratins.* ❧

1. Set the stock in a saucepan over medium-high heat and keep warm.

2. As the stock is warming up, heat the oil in a wide sauté pan. Add the garlic and onion and cook over medium heat for 2 minutes, until fragrant, stirring

regularly to avoid coloring. Add the pasta and stir constantly for 2 minutes. Add just enough stock to cover the pasta, and lower the heat to medium-low. Cover and simmer for 10 minutes, stirring from time to time and adding more stock when it is absorbed. Five minutes into the cooking, add the zucchini and season with salt and pepper.

3. Taste the pasta for doneness. If it isn't quite done and all the liquids have been absorbed, add a little more stock (or water if you're out of stock), cover, and cook for a few more minutes. Repeat until you've reached an al dente consistency; the total cooking time will depend on the type of pasta you used. Adjust the seasoning, transfer into bowls or plates, sprinkle with cacao nibs and Parmesan, and serve immediately.

6 cups stock or filtered water

3 tablespoons extra virgin olive oil

3 garlic cloves, minced

1 medium yellow onion, finely chopped

14 ounces dried short pasta, such as ricciole, penne, or fusilli

4 small zucchini, cut into sticks or thin slices with a mandoline or a sharp knife

Fine sea salt and freshly ground pepper

2 tablespoons cacao nibs (not chocolate-coated), toasted in a dry skillet and coarsely crushed (substitute $1/4$ cup pine nuts, toasted)

Aged Parmesan, coarsely grated

Serves 4 as a main course (the recipe can be halved)

POULET MIJOTÉ À LA MOUTARDE

Mustard Chicken Stew

*S*tews are your best ally for stress-free dinner parties. They will simmer away unattended on the stove, their juices concentrating and their flavors deepening while you chat with your friends. They don't really mind how long they cook, and they will in fact get better if you forget about them a little — not too much, though, or they will get upset and scorch your pot. They are also great to feed a crowd, and I usually size my stews for a couple more servings than I think I'll need, so I can accommodate a last-minute guest and enjoy the leftovers the next day.

This chicken stew is made mostly from pantry items, which makes it quite convenient for a weeknight dinner. The chicken cooks slowly in a sauce of red onions, tomatoes, and old-fashioned mustard, until the meat is so tender it falls off the bones without being prompted. I serve it over rice or pasta with roasted garlic paste, an emphatically flavored and low-maintenance condiment that softens in the oven while you prepare the stew.

For my fresh chicken needs I turn to the butcher shop around the corner, where Mario the butcher cleans and cuts it for me as we engage in good-natured banter. This usually involves him asking what's for dinner and what time he should show up, his wife rolling her eyes behind the register, and me laughing my way out of this delicate situation. You can also keep chicken parts in the freezer and use those instead.

1 whole head garlic

Extra virgin olive oil

Fine sea salt and freshly ground pepper

One 3- to 3^1/2-pound whole free-range chicken, cut in 8 serving pieces (2 breasts, 2 thighs, 2 wings, and 2 drumsticks, with bones and skin), thawed if frozen

6 medium red onions, about 2 pounds

One 28- to 32-ounce can good-quality whole peeled tomatoes, drained

1 tablespoon fresh thyme or 1^1/2 teaspoons dried thyme

2 bay leaves

A good pinch of ground chile powder

^{1}/3 cup dry white wine

3 tablespoons old-fashioned Dijon mustard with whole mustard seeds (substitute ^{1}/4 cup regular Dijon mustard)

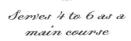

Serves 4 to 6 as a main course

1. Preheat the oven to 400°F.

2. Peel the outer layers of skin from the head of garlic until you reach the individual cloves. Slice off the top of the head so the flesh of each clove is exposed. Put the head of garlic on a sheet of foil, drizzle with olive oil, season with salt and pepper, and close the foil into a pouch. Bake for 45 minutes, until the flesh of each clove is light brown and very soft when tested with the tip of a knife.

3. Once you've slipped the garlic into the oven, heat 1 teaspoon olive oil over medium heat in a large heavy pot or Dutch oven. Working in two batches, arrange the chicken in the pot, skin side down, in a single layer. Season with salt and pepper and cook for 3 minutes on each side, until golden. (Be careful not to burn yourself with the sizzling chicken fat.)

4. While the chicken is browning, peel and quarter the onions. Set the meat aside on a plate and pour out the excess chicken fat. Put the onions in the pot and cook for 5 minutes, until softened, stirring regularly.

5. Add the tomatoes, thyme, bay leaves, and ground chile powder, and arrange the chicken over the vegetables. Pour in the wine and bring to a simmer. Cover and cook

over medium-low heat for 40 minutes, stirring from time to time to make sure the vegetables don't stick to the bottom.

6. Remove the garlic from the oven, open the pouch, and let stand until cool enough to handle. Squeeze the garlic out of each clove into a small bowl, and mash with a fork to form a paste. Taste and adjust the seasoning. Cover and set aside.

7. When the chicken is cooked, spoon the mustard in the pot and stir to blend into the sauce. Turn the heat up to medium-high and cook uncovered for 10 minutes, stirring regularly, until the sauce is thick enough to cling to the meat. Taste the sauce and adjust the seasoning.

8. Cover and keep over low heat until ready to serve. Serve over rice or pasta (fish out the bay leaves, or simply tell your dining companions not to eat them), with garlic paste on the side. The stew and garlic can be prepared up to a day ahead, covered, and refrigerated. Reheat the stew over gentle heat, and bring the garlic paste to room temperature before serving. The leftover sauce from the stew is splendid on pasta.

*W*INE DOMAINE GARRIGUE "CUVÉE ROMAINE" 2003 CÔTES DU RHÔNE (France, Côtes du Rhône, red) This Côtes du Rhône is less intensely fruity than most, with a nose of blackberry, herbs, and fennel. It is a medium-bodied wine with tart cherry flavors and earthy, spicy notes. It has a food-friendly acidity, lightly gripping tannins, and a dry finish.

TARTARE AU COUTEAU

Hand-cut Steak Tartare

*W*hen I feel particularly ravenous, it is often steak tartare that calls my name — perhaps I should check my iron levels. Luckily, it is a dish that is widely served in Parisian restaurants, so my hunger for rarer-than-rare meat is easily satisfied.

Pâtes par Absorption, Courgette & Cacao
Cacao and Zucchini Absorption Pasta, page 102

Boulettes d'Agneau aux Pruneaux
Lamb and Prune Meatballs, page 109

3 tablespoons strong Dijon mustard

3 tablespoons Worcestershire sauce

1 teaspoon Tabasco sauce

3 tablespoons ketchup

1 tablespoon brandy (optional, but highly recommended)

3 medium shallots, finely chopped

3 garlic cloves, finely chopped

3 tablespoons small capers (if you can find only large capers, chop them roughly)

2 tablespoons chopped fresh flat-leaf parsley leaves

1 tablespoon chopped fresh tarragon leaves

$1/3$ cup shelled hazelnuts, toasted and roughly chopped — discard the pieces of brown skin that come loose in the process (optional)

$1^1/2$ pounds extra-fresh high-quality beef fillet — filet mignon or Chateaubriand (let the vendor know you plan on eating it raw)

4 egg yolks from extra-fresh high-quality medium eggs

Fleur de sel or kosher salt

Freshly ground pepper

Serves 4 as a main course

Ordering steak tartare does require a certain amount of trust in the kitchen, since raw meat should be handled with the greatest of care. Two phrases to look for on a French menu are *tartare minute* and *au couteau:* this means that the meat is prepared right to order and chopped by hand, which gives it less time for unfortunate encounters with bacteria, and a more satisfying bite.

Steak tartare is very easy to make at home, and it will give a classy bistro touch to your meal, served with thick-cut fries and a salad of mixed greens. Use nothing but the best quality of meat and eggs, and, of course, make sure your guests are comfortable with raw meat. As a textural twist, I like to add a handful of chopped hazelnuts to my steak tartare, but this is optional.

NOTE For food safety, clean your hands and tools thoroughly before and after handling raw meat.

1. In a small bowl, whisk together the mustard, Worcestershire sauce, Tabasco, ketchup, and brandy, if using. In another bowl, combine the shallots, garlic, capers, herbs, and hazelnuts, if using. This can be prepared up to an hour ahead.

2. At the very last minute, chop the meat into $1/4$-inch dice (not too fine) using a large sharp knife. In a medium mixing bowl, combine the meat, egg yolks, and mustard mixture with a fork. Season with salt and pepper. Fold in the shallot mixture and blend well.

3. Divide the meat in four equal portions and arrange them in patties on serving plates (use cylindrical molds if you have them). Serve immediately, with ad-

ditional mustard, Worcestershire sauce, Tabasco, ketchup, salt, and pepper on the table for each guest to adjust the seasoning.

VARIATION The seasoned meat patties can be pan-seared briefly on each side. This is called a steak tartare *aller-retour* — literally, return ticket.

*W*INE CHÂTEAU GREYSAC MÉDOC 2001 (France, Bordeaux, red) The bold flavors of steak tartare call for a Bordeaux: medium-bodied and with lower tannins than you might expect, this one presents a typical nose of black cherry, toasty cedar, and spice, and these flavors extend on the palate in a straightforward way.

FOOD SAFETY *Consuming raw eggs presents a very slight risk of food poisoning, due to their possible contamination by salmonella. The risk is greatly reduced if you use extra-fresh, clean eggs with an intact shell, refrigerate them properly, and carefully avoid contact between the outside of the shell and the inside of the egg. In any case, you should not serve raw eggs to young children, pregnant women, the elderly, or the ill.* ✿

BOULETTES D'AGNEAU AUX PRUNEAUX

Lamb and Prune Meatballs

*I*t has been brought to my attention that the prune is often on the receiving end of contempt or mockery in North America, and I feel I must step up in defense of this marvelous dried fruit, which does not pale one bit in comparison to its more popular cousins the fig and the apricot.

Prunes are much more treasured in France, where they are often paired with such nobility as chocolate, Armagnac, duck, or guinea fowl. The most prized variety comes from the city of Agen: its production can be traced back to a monastery in the thirteenth century, and locals are so proud of their prune that they have founded a brotherhood of knights to serve its cause, la Compagnie des Chevaliers du Pruneau d'Agen.

FRESHLY DRIED FRUIT *Even though dried fruits have a long shelf life, it is worth seeking out freshly dried specimens. A good prune should be black, wrinkled, and shiny; it should be plump but not too soft, moist but not sticky.* ✿

Gastronomes Gastronomic brotherhoods have been founded all over France to celebrate and protect local specialties, either food (*confréries gourmandes*) or wine (*confréries bachiques*). Most were created over the past fifty years, but their approach is resolutely old-fashioned, based on all-but-forgotten traditions. Each brotherhood has a board of dignitaries (with such honorific titles as grand master, grand chancellor, and grand constable), and members have special apparel to wear (a cape or a robe, a funny hat, and symbolic accessories hung on a belt or as a medallion). They work year-round to promote their beloved specialty and gather for a yearly reunion, during which the product is feted and new members are sworn in. I hope to have that honor someday, though I can't decide if it's the banquet or the outfit I most covet.

I myself adore the gentle sweetness of prunes, their unassuming look, and their velvety flesh. I use them in desserts, like a soup with spiced red wine or a hearty *far aux pruneaux*, but also in savory dishes, such as these aromatic meatballs. They are quick to assemble and make for a reviving meal, served with fluffy couscous and a cup of Greek-style yogurt for dipping.

1. In a medium mixing bowl, combine the meat, prunes, shallots, garlic, parsley, orange zest, allspice, egg, the 1 tablespoon olive oil, the salt, and pepper. Mix well with a fork. Cover and refrigerate for 30 minutes, or up to 8 hours. (If you don't have that kind of time, refrigerate for just 10 minutes.)

2. Remove the bowl from the refrigerator. Wash your hands well, and keep them damp. Scoop out rounded tablespoons of the mixture and roll them into balls between your palms. Set aside in a single layer on two plates until you've used up all the meat. Wash your hands thoroughly again.

1 pound ground lamb meat, preferably from the shoulder

12 good-quality prunes, sometimes called dried plums, pitted and finely chopped

2 small shallots, finely chopped

1 garlic clove, finely chopped

$1/4$ cup (packed) fresh flat-leaf parsley leaves, finely chopped, plus a few for garnish

1 tablespoon (packed) freshly grated and finely minced orange zest, from about 2 organic oranges

$1/4$ teaspoon allspice

1 large egg, lightly beaten

1 tablespoon plus 1 teaspoon extra virgin olive oil

$1/2$ teaspoon fine sea salt

$1/4$ teaspoon freshly ground pepper

Serves 4 as a main course, 6 as a starter
Chilling time: 30 minutes

3. Heat 1 teaspoon olive oil in a large nonstick skillet over medium heat. Add half of the meatballs in a single layer without crowding. Cook for 8 to 10 minutes, stirring the meatballs gently around the pan to brown them all over. Set aside on a clean plate and cover with foil while you cook the second batch. Return the first batch to the pan, cover, and reheat for 2 minutes. Transfer to a serving dish, sprinkle with parsley, and serve with couscous and Greek-style yogurt.

VARIATION If you don't have the patience to shape balls, make 4 to 6 patties.

WINE HÉRITAGE DU RHÔNE CÔTES DU RHÔNE 2003 (France, Côtes du Rhône, red) Côtes du Rhône is a reliable pairing for lamb. This one has intense flavors of blackberry and black currant, with spicy notes of black pepper and cinnamon. It has medium tannins that cut through the richness of the lamb and a well-rounded finish.

Dîner

DINNER PARTY

Ceviche Fraise Avocat
STRAWBERRY AVOCADO CEVICHE

*Saint-Jacques à la Mangue,
Tuile au Parmesan*
SEA SCALLOPS AND MANGO WITH
PARMESAN WAFER

Soufflés au Comté
COMTÉ CHEESE SOUFFLÉS

Tagine d'Agneau aux Poires
LAMB TAGINE WITH PEARS

Courgettes Rondes Farcies au Boulgour
BULGUR-STUFFED ROUND ZUCCHINI

Bœuf Bourguignon
BEEF BOURGUIGNON

Carbonades Flamandes
FLEMISH CARBONADES

*A*lthough this was never established as an official rule between us, Maxence usually lets me mastermind the menu for our dinner parties: he knows how rhapsodically I throw myself into the process, and he is content to act as the consulting voice. A week or so before the set date, I start toying with ideas. This is the most thrilling part of the entire process, when anything's possible and I get to dream about the quintessential meal, search for ideal pairings, and doodle plating sketches.

Inspiration may spring from a newly acquired ingredient or tool, a seasonal product I'm excited about, or a restaurant dish I've recently tasted. A few directions emerge and I jot them down in a notebook. If I need additional layers of inspiration, I build a fort on the couch with piles of cookbooks, clippings, and past notes, and I sift through them, pencil in hand.

When I have enough ideas to play with, I try to coax them into a sound ensemble, tweaking some and discarding others — however painful that is — and thinking in terms of:

Seasonality. If you focus on ingredients and preparations that are tailored to the season and the weather, the resulting meal will magically be what your guests are in the mood for; the ingredients will be easy to find and at their most rewarding stage of ripeness. Of course, if you live in a place like Paris, where the seasons like to play tricks on you, pretending spring has arrived only to abruptly dive back into the depths of winter, you may find yourself serving a cool asparagus salad to shawl-wrapped friends. That can't be helped, and the asparagus will taste fine regardless.

Variety and harmony. The different dishes of a meal are like the movements of a concerto: they should complement each other flatteringly, lending a smooth flow to the meal, but they should offer enough diversity to surprise and entertain. Harmony comes naturally when you heed the seasonality advice, and it is helpful to consider regional and cultural affinity as well.

Simplicity. The most successful meals I've ever enjoyed, the ones that have made the longest-lasting impression on me, were a judicious combination of excellent products and simple preparations. This is no small feat — clutter is much easier to achieve — but it is to be strived for.

Lightness. It's not that I want to play health coach to my friends; I just don't want them (or myself, for that matter) to feel too full too soon. If the main dish is on the rich side, I'll lighten up the first course and prepare a fruit-based dessert. If I want to serve an indulgent chocolate tart, it probably shouldn't follow a cheese fondue. And if the main course has a starchy side, the starter will be lush with greens.

Practicality. For every labor-intensive dish, I go the easy route on another. I try to identify what can be made ahead of time and avoid dishes that require frantic last-minute cooking. I check that the workload can be divided between the stovetop and the oven, and that I won't need the same cooking dish for two different preparations.

Guests' preferences. For most of my friends, I can tell if they have adventurous tastes, if they have the appetite of a wolf or a sparrow, if they tend to avoid red meat, or if a hazelnut might kill them. If we have guests we don't know very well, I assume they will let me know of any life-threatening food intolerances, and plan an easy-to-like, conservative menu, steering clear of unusual pairings or acquired-taste ingredients — sea urchin, tripe, that sort of thing.

Experimentation. Common sense might sternly advise you against trying new recipes when you have company, but I have to say I happily disregard this warning. A large part of my pleasure as a cook is to invent dishes for my friends to taste, and frankly, who has time for trial runs? I do however choose my guinea pigs carefully — prospective employers and world leaders don't qualify. More important, I listen to my gut feeling and only attempt novel preparations if I am reasonably confident that they won't result in a resounding catastrophe. And if they do, I figure it will make a good story for the grandkids.

When I'm happy with the drafted menu, I run it by Maxence to get his thoughts and draw up two lists. The first one is a broad-stroked breakdown of the different cooking steps grouped together by time, to get an idea of the workload. If this reveals that my menu is too ambitious, putting me at a high risk for hysteria when dinnertime comes around, I'll go back to the drawing board to streamline it. The second list is simply a shopping list of the ingredients I'll need, arranged by provider and by day (the cheese can be purchased a few days in advance, but one of us will hop out to the bakery in late afternoon to get fresh bread).

Sometimes the menu is simple enough that I don't need to write the first list on paper — the different steps can just be laid out in my mind — but I have found that the shopping list is vital. If you've ever found yourself in the kitchen, desperately looking for that key ingredient you've forgotten to buy and trying hard to wish it into existence, you know it doesn't work too well.

As the date gets closer, the menu often shifts from the original plan: a shinier, too-good-to-pass-up idea may fall into my lap, or I won't be able to find this or that ingredient and curse the skies before moving on, or maybe I'll realize as I cook that things don't seem to turn out quite the way they should, and I'll have to adapt.

MENU OUTLINE

The structure of our meals is largely open to variations and shortcuts depending on our resources of time and energy, but the basic outline is this:

Apéro/**Apéritif.** French etiquette requires that guests arrive fifteen minutes after the appointed time: this is called *le quart d'heure de politesse*, and it gives the hosts a margin of error in their planning, or time to rest their feet a little. My generation seems to take that advice very much to heart, upping the ante to thirty minutes or even an hour, but we are quite relaxed about this (especially since we're chronically late ourselves), and we just go about our business, with drinks and small bites at the ready to welcome our friends as they show up, in their own good time. (See page 73 for more on apéritif.)

Once everyone has arrived, settled down, and the appetizer platter has been polished off, we make a collective move to the table. "Where should we sit?" our guests ask. "Wherever you like!" we reply. Our dinner parties are casual enough that we don't need to follow any of the official seating rules, but for practical reasons I will pick a chair that gives me access to the kitchen without having to climb over anyone.

Entrée/**Starter.** Confusingly enough, the word *entrée* means "first course" in French, not "main course." A starter should be something small that doesn't fill you up, yet offers enough flavor to tease the taste buds and make them stamp their feet for more. It can be a salad, a slice of terrine with cornichons and good bread, a refreshing seafood dish, a lightly sophisticated soup . . . Or, as a shortcut, you can make the apéritif spread a bit more substantial and forgo the first course altogether.

Plat/**Main course.** For the main part of the meal, I favor stewed or baked dishes that require little last-minute work and are flexible as to the time of serving. I will slip them in the oven or begin to reheat them as we get started on the first course, and finish them up whenever we're ready for them. I typically serve the main dish with just one side (see page 137) and plenty of fresh bread. Depending on the type of preparation, the first and main courses are either plated in the kitchen or served family style from a dish brought to the table. Individual plating looks classier, but it makes hot food go cold faster, so I don't let fancy get in the way of tasty.

Fromage/**Cheese.** After the main course we ask, somewhat rhetorically, if anyone would like a bit of cheese. Two categories of diners can be identified at that precise moment: those who shake their heads politely and pass ("Oh no, I couldn't possibly"), and those whose eyes light up and sparkle, revealing unsuspected resources of appetite. In my experience, the keenness of the latter spreads like wildfire to the former, who will join in the fun as soon as the cheese platter appears.

Dessert. We take a longer break after the cheese course for everyone to regain his senses before moving on to sweets. If dessert is something that is shared, like a tart or a cake, I cut smallish servings: not everyone has as much appetite for desserts as I do, and I'd rather see my sweet-toothed friends go for seconds than have the others struggle bravely to finish what's on their plates.

It is quite accepted in France to serve a dessert that was purchased at a *pâtisserie*: a cake, a tart, or an assortment of individual confections. The art of the host is seen in the informed choice of the purveyor and the tasteful selection of pastries. Since I love baking I wouldn't dream of passing up a chance to play with my whisks and spatulas, but it's nice to know one has the option.

Café et mignardises/**Coffee and sweets.** The meal ends with cups of tea or coffee; if our neighbors are dining with us, they will disappear next door and brew espressos in their nifty percolator. I also bring small sweets to nibble on as we drink, either on one little plate or on the saucer of each cup. This can be something as effortless as squares of dark chocolate or miniature *macarons* from the pastry shop, or it can be homemade *mignardises* if I've had time to plan for them (see page 217). I have a particular fondness for this unexpected encore to the meal, and the way it mirrors the appetizer bites that opened the evening.

At this point, Maxence may also suggest a drop of *digestif*, such as an old Cognac or Armagnac, and this offer is usually greeted with much enthusiasm — especially by our male guests.

A Few Things to Keep in Mind

Shortcuts. While I urge you not to cut corners on the quality of your ingredients, you can save time and energy by making the most of the specialty stores you have access to. An entire appetizer platter can be assembled with products from the deli; a terrine from the butcher's or a piece of smoked salmon can serve as a fine first course, with a few condiments and accessories; and if you have no time or inclination to make dessert, the pastry shop is your best friend. I am not suggesting you create an entire meal from these shortcuts — it would seem discourteous — but if you mix them cleverly with your own cooking, they can bail you out for one course or another.

Small servings. When you prepare a multicourse dinner, you want your guests to be able to enjoy it fully and not stall halfway through: it's best to serve reasonable portions at first, then offer seconds.

Pace yourself. Take the time to savor the meal. A little pause between each course is welcome, so everyone can sit back and enjoy the lingering flavors of the previous dish. This also gives you time to put the finishing touches on what comes next.

Let people help you. Some of the guests may volunteer to give you a hand, bring dishes to the table, or clear plates. Interestingly enough, the initial impulse of the well-mannered French host is to decline. But if the offer is sincere (sometimes people just *say* that) and you do need a bit of help, I recommend accepting gracefully: it makes your assistants feel part of the team, and it lightens your workload considerably.

Don't set the bar too high. It is very commendable to push yourself and do your best, but you have nothing to prove, and your guests are coming for a home-cooked meal. However exhilarating it is to emulate restaurant-style dishes and plating, the spirit of your cooking should remain playful: sometimes things work out beautifully and sometimes they don't, but don't put your honor on the line. The crux of the matter is to enjoy yourself, bask in the company of your friends, and invest the exact amount of time you feel comfortable with.

CEVICHE FRAISE AVOCAT

Strawberry Avocado Ceviche

$\mathcal{C}$eviche is a superb warm weather starter, light and refreshing: it is a specialty from Latin America, in which raw fish is cubed and marinated in citrus juices. The acidity of the marinade "cooks" the fish while preserving its moistness and lends it high-pitched notes. I like to balance this tartness with softer, sweeter flavors, and I am very fond of this avocado and strawberry combo. Ceviche will look particularly dashing if you serve it in transparent glasses, to showcase its colors.

1. Remove any remaining bone from the fish with tweezers. Cut the fish in $^1/_3$-inch cubes and transfer to a medium glass or ceramic baking dish. Add the citrus juices, olive oil, and Tabasco. Season with salt and pepper; toss to coat. Cover with plastic wrap and refrigerate for 2 to 6 hours, stirring halfway through. Set a fine-mesh sieve over a bowl. Remove the fish from the refrigerator, pour it into the sieve, and let it drain, reserving the juices, as you prepare the other ingredients.

2. Rinse the strawberries, pat them dry, and hull them. Cut in $^1/_3$-inch pieces and combine with the honey, tossing gently to coat. Cut the avocado in half, remove the pit, and dice the flesh in $^1/_3$-inch pieces.

3. In a medium mixing bowl, combine the fish, strawberries, avocado, and chervil, and toss gently. Taste and adjust the seasoning. Divide among glasses, pour in a tablespoon of the reserved juices, and decorate with a

14 ounces extra-fresh fillets lean firm fish, such as mahi-mahi, swordfish, or halibut (let the vendor know that the fish will be marinated, not cooked)

2 tablespoons lime juice, from about $^1/_2$ lime

$^1/_2$ cup lemon juice, from about 2 lemons

1 tablespoon extra virgin olive oil

1 to 2 teaspoons Tabasco sauce

Fleur de sel or kosher salt

Freshly ground pepper

$1^1/_2$ cups fresh strawberries, plus 4 small ones for garnish, about 1 pint total

1 tablespoon mild honey

1 medium avocado

2 tablespoons (packed) fresh chervil leaves (substitute flat-leaf parsley or cilantro leaves)

Serves 4 as a starter
Chilling time: 2 hours

strawberry. Serve immediately, or chill for up to 4 hours (remove from the refrigerator 15 minutes before serving).

*W*INE BOUVET BRUT ROSÉ NV (France, Loire, sparkling rosé) The crispness of this sparkler matches the acidity of the fish and cuts through the richness of the avocado, while the berry flavors respond to the strawberry component. It has a clean finish and a light-to-medium body, ideal to open a meal.

***

SAINT-JACQUES À LA MANGUE, TUILE AU PARMESAN

Sea Scallops and Mango with Parmesan Wafer

*S*erving scallops is the quickest and most delicious way to turn an ordinary dinner party into a classy, sparkling affair. Foie gras and caviar set the tone quite efficiently, too, but there is something more refined about the scallop, less obvious perhaps, that makes it a French classic for festive meals — most suitably during the winter months, when the opalescent mollusks are in season.

Fish markets in France sell sea scallops live and in the shell, an undisputable sign of freshness. If you so desire, the man with a plastic apron in the back will shuck them for you, at lightning speed and no additional charge. But a chef and friend of mine once taught me how to do this myself, and Maxence and I have been opening and cleaning our own scallops ever since. This makes us feel proudly self-sufficient for all of thirty minutes, and it allows us to cut the shucking line at the shop, too.

I generally serve sea scallops as a first course: since they are delicate in taste and not very filling, they play that role admirably. Three per guest is a good number, and a trio of sea scallops will look attractive regardless of your plating skills.

Scallops taste best in the simplest of preparations. Some argue that raw is the best, if not the only way to go. If you're 100 percent sure of the pristine freshness of your scallops, thinly slice them, season them with salt, pepper, and a drizzle of olive oil, and enjoy your snow-white carpaccio.

I do like raw scallops, but I prefer a brief searing in a bit of butter. This crowns both ends of the scallops with a thin golden crust, while their hearts remain pale pink and translucent: their meaty texture is thus intact, and the full bouquet of their flavors preserved. (When brutally overcooked, scallops turn into depressing, rubbery versions of themselves; the only upside is that they will bounce lightly when thrown against a hard surface.)

Because they are subtly sweet, scallops have a particular affinity to such vegetables as leeks, artichokes, beets, or caramelized onions. But the one that makes my palate tap-dance with glee, is with the mango. In the following dish, this partnership is rounded by a bit of cilantro, a squeeze of lime juice, and a lacy Parmesan wafer.

1. **Prepare the Parmesan wafers.** Combine $1/4$ cup of the grated Parmesan (reserve the remaining cheese) with the flour in a small bowl. On the left half of a large nonstick skillet, pour 1 tablespoon of the cheese mixture, and use the back of the measuring spoon to spread it into a thin disk, about $3^1/2$ inches in diameter. Repeat with another tablespoon of the cheese mixture, setting it on the right half of the skillet so the two disks don't touch. Set the skillet over high heat until the cheese is bubbly and is just starting to turn golden. Remove from heat and let cool for 30 seconds. Using a thin spatula, loosen the disks cautiously from the skillet, and transfer onto a rolling pin to give them a curved shape, working quickly so the wafers won't have time to harden. Let cool completely. Rinse the skillet under cold water to cool it down, wipe it dry, and repeat to make two more wafers.

2. In a small mixing bowl, combine the mango with the remaining cheese, lime juice, and cilantro leaves. Season with salt and pepper, and set aside.

3. Melt the butter in the skillet over medium-high heat. Set the scallops upright in the pan and cook for 3 minutes (1 minute for bay scallops) without disturbing them, un-

$3/4$ cup freshly and finely grated Parmesan, about 3 ounces (choose a relatively young, moist Parmesan; if it is aged, it will be too dry to melt properly for the wafers)

$1^1/2$ teaspoons all-purpose flour

$1^1/3$ cups diced mango, from about 1 large ripe mango

$1/2$ teaspoon freshly squeezed lime juice

$1/4$ cup (lightly packed) fresh cilantro leaves, plus 4 stems for garnish (substitute fresh flat-leaf parsley leaves)

Fleur de sel or kosher salt

Freshly ground pepper

2 tablespoons unsalted butter

12 sea scallops, thawed if frozen (see page 122), or substitute 10 ounces bay scallops

———— ❊ ————

Serves 4 as a starter

Scallops The sea scallop is a mollusk that lives in a light pink, fan-shaped shell, not very spacious but ingeniously organized and decorated with flair. The edible part, about $1^1/2$ inches in diameter, is the muscle that holds both sides of the shell together. Bay scallops belong to the same family. They are much smaller, about half an inch, but can be substituted for sea scallops and vice versa (three or four bay scallops for one sea scallop). On the U.S. market, bay scallops are scarcer than sea scallops and cost a little more, but they are considered more delicate. It is the opposite in France, where the large variety, called *coquille Saint-Jacques*, is far more prized — and pricier — than the tiny *pétoncle*. Buy your scallops fresh if possible, from a fish market that has a good turnover. Look for firm scallops with a dewy sheen and a sweet, not seaweedy, smell. Store in the refrigerator and use within a day or two. You can also use frozen scallops; thawed scallops are chewier than fresh, but you'll live.

til a golden crust forms at the bottom. Flip the scallops with locking tongs and cook for 2 to 3 more minutes (1 minute for bay scallops). The top and bottom of the scallops should be opaque, but the center should remain translucent.

4. Divide the mango mixture among four plates, arranging it to form a round layer. Top with three sea scallops (or a fourth of the bay scallops) and a Parmesan wafer. Garnish with a stem of cilantro and serve immediately.

*W*INE GUY SAGET VOUVRAY 2004 (France, Loire, white) This Vouvray is fresh and fruity, with peach, honey, and crisp apple flavors joined by hints of pineapple and mango. It is slightly sweet, to flatter the mango and scallops, but its acidity keeps it from being heavy, or cloying.

SOUFFLÉS AU COMTÉ

Comté Cheese Soufflés

*S*oufflés are cursed with a paralyzingly intimidating reputation, and many cooks have been led to believe it would be pure folly to so much as consider serving them to company, as if the universe was threatening to collapse at the same time as their soufflé tops.

Let us demystify the whole thing, shall we? First of all, soufflés are not that difficult to make: you just need to measure all the ingredients beforehand, and read the instructions carefully (half the audience gets up and leaves the room). Second, soufflés don't have to be an entirely last-minute operation: you do need to bake them just before serving, but I've had good success preparing the batter up to two hours in advance. Perhaps they don't rise quite as much, but really, the naked eye can't tell the difference. And more to the point, the one thing experts forget to mention is that fallen soufflés are just as delectable as their puffy counterparts — in fact, I find them even more charming, in that I'm-not-perfect-but-neither-are-you kind of way.

4 tablespoons (^{1}/2 stick) unsalted butter,
plus 1 tablespoon to grease the
ramekins

1 cup freshly grated Comté, about 3^1/2
ounces (substitute Gruyère)

^{1}/3 cup all-purpose flour

1 cup milk (not skim)

4 large egg yolks, lightly beaten

^{1}/2 teaspoon fine sea salt

^{1}/4 teaspoon freshly ground pepper

Freshly grated nutmeg (use a whole
nutmeg and a fine grater)

3 large egg whites

Serves 6 as a starter

1. Measure all your ingredients before you start. Grease six 6-ounce ramekins with 1 tablespoon butter. Make sure you don't touch the inside surface once it's buttered, or the soufflés won't rise as well. Sprinkle the bottom of the ramekins with 1 teaspoon grated cheese each (reserve the remaining cheese), shake the ramekins lightly to coat the bottom and sides, and place them in the refrigerator.

2. Preheat the oven to 400°F (unless you are preparing the batter in advance).

3. Melt the remaining 4 tablespoons butter in a 3-quart saucepan over medium-high heat. Add the flour all at once, and whisk it into the butter (this is called a *roux blanc*). Cook for 2 minutes, whisking continually. Add the milk and whisk quickly to incorporate, making sure you don't leave any clumps on the bottom and sides of the pan. The mixture will thicken. At the first boil, remove from heat. (If this is the first time you do this, let me congratulate you: you have just made a béchamel!)

4. Let the béchamel cool for 2 minutes. Add the egg yolks, whisking continually to prevent them from cooking, and season with ^{1}/4 teaspoon of the salt, the freshly ground pepper, and a dash of nutmeg. Reserve 3 tablespoons of the remaining grated cheese in a small bowl and fold the rest into the béchamel mixture.

5. In a medium mixing bowl, combine the egg whites and the remaining ^{1}/4 teaspoon salt. Use an electric whisk to beat the egg whites until stiff. (This will take 3 to 4 minutes at high speed. To know if the egg whites are ready, lift the beaters out of the bowl: the egg whites in the bowl should form a rounded peak that doesn't collapse.)

6. Spoon one third of the egg whites into the béchamel mixture, and stir with a spatula to blend. Fold in the rest of the egg whites very gently, lifting the béchamel mixture up and over the egg whites with the spatula, until all of the egg whites are

Soufflés au Comté
Comté Cheese Soufflés

incorporated. (The batter can be prepared up to 2 hours in advance — cover tightly and refrigerate. Preheat the oven to 400°F 10 to 15 minutes before baking.)

7. Remove the ramekins from the fridge and place them on a baking sheet. Divide the soufflé batter among the ramekins (they won't be filled to the top). Sprinkle with the reserved grated cheese and bake for 12 to 15 minutes, until puffed up and golden (don't open the oven door during the first 12 minutes or you'll be sorry). Serve immediately, with a salad of young greens.

VARIATIONS Add 1 tablespoon paprika to the flour, or 2 teaspoons sweet smoked Spanish paprika (see page 29), or 2 teaspoons curry powder, or 1 ounce dried mushrooms, ground to a fine powder.

WINE E. GUIGAL 2002 CÔTES DU RHÔNE BLANC (France, Côtes du Rhône, white) This blend offers flavors of citrus, ripe peach, and fig, with hints of almond and spice. Bone-dry and refreshing, it is mineral, with a good body and acidity.

TAGINE D'AGNEAU AUX POIRES

Lamb Tagine with Pears

When I was eight years old, my family moved into an apartment that was around the corner from a fine Moroccan restaurant. It became a favorite destination for last-minute dinner arrangements with friends of my parents' — the restaurant had an impressive display of stuffed reptiles that kept us kids endlessly entertained — and on summer days, when the wind was blowing in the right direction, my appetite was teased by the caramelized barbecued smells seeping in through my open window.

While my preference in those days went to the safe combo of chicken, couscous, and stewed vegetables, I have since developed a keen taste for the wide range of flavors that Moroccan cuisine has to offer: elegant and generous, it always promises to whisk you and your taste buds away on an exotic voyage.

RAS EL HANOUT *If you're at all excited about Moroccan cooking, you may want to add ras el hanout, a complex mix of spices that enters the preparation of many traditional dishes, to your spice rack. Most bottled mixes are made with just a handful of spices, but an authentic one will boast at least twenty-four, and up to fifty. I buy mine from a Moroccan restaurant in Paris, where it is freshly made and knockout flavorful. If you are able to find ras el hanout, use 2 teaspoons in this recipe, in place of the cumin, ground cinnamon, ginger, nutmeg, and pepper.* ❧

Tagine is the name given to a variety of spice-rich stews made with meat (lamb, veal, or chicken), vegetables, and often fruits and nuts. It is also the name of the dome-shaped clay dish in which those stews are traditionally baked, but a good heavy pot does the job quite adequately. Some tagine recipes have you set the pot in the oven, but I prefer the stovetop method: it makes it easier to check on the progress of your stew as you lift the lid, breathe in the sumptuous smells, wait for the steam on your glasses to subside, and give the meat a few stirs of encouragement.

The following recipe features lamb, cooked slowly with onions and plenty of spices. Served with tender pears and toasted almonds, it is a lovely fall or winter dish that gently combines sweet and savory flavors. As is true of most stews, the longer a tagine cooks, the tastier it will be; it is recommended to make it a day ahead. And although a tagine is normally served by itself or with rounds of soft flat bread, I like it with a side of couscous, to soak up the juices.

1. Heat the olive oil over medium heat in a large heavy pot or Dutch oven. Arrange half of the meat in a single layer over the bottom of the pot without crowding. Cook for 4 minutes on each side, until the meat starts to brown. Season with salt, set aside on a plate, and repeat with the remaining pieces of meat.

2. While the meat is browning, peel and slice the onions. Peel and mince the garlic. Once all the meat is browned and set aside, combine the onions, garlic, and 1 tablespoon water in the pot. Cook over medium heat for 10 minutes, until softened, stirring regularly. Add the meat, sprinkle with the spices (from saffron to ground chile powder), stir, and cook for 2 minutes, until fragrant. Pour in hot water halfway up the meat. Bring to a simmer, cover, and lower the heat to medium-low. Cook for 2 hours, stirring every once in a while, until the meat is very tender.

1 tablespoon extra virgin olive oil

2¹/2 pounds boneless lamb shoulder, cut in 1-inch cubes and patted dry with paper towels

Fine sea salt

1 pound yellow onions, about 3 medium

2 garlic cloves

A pinch of saffron threads

¹/2 teaspoon whole cumin seeds

¹/2 teaspoon ground cinnamon

¹/2 teaspoon ground ginger

¹/4 teaspoon freshly grated nutmeg (use a whole nutmeg and a fine grater)

¹/4 teaspoon freshly ground pepper

A good pinch of ground chile powder

³/4 cup whole blanched almonds

1 tablespoon unsalted butter

4 ripe pears, about 2 pounds, peeled, cored and quartered — choose a variety that will retain its shape when cooked, such as Bosc, Winter Nellis, or Anjou

Serves 6 as a main course

3. While the meat is simmering, toast the almonds in a large dry skillet until golden and fragrant, and set aside. In the same skillet, melt the butter over medium heat until it starts to sizzle. Add the quartered pears and toss gently to coat. Lower the heat to medium-low, cover, and cook for 12 minutes, until the pears are cooked through and slightly translucent. Keep warm.

4. Remove the lid from the pot, turn the heat up to medium-high, and cook uncovered for 10 to 15 minutes, stirring regularly, until the sauce is thick enough to cling to the meat. Taste the sauce and adjust the seasoning. Transfer the meat and sauce to a serving dish. Surround with the pears, sprinkle with toasted almonds, and serve with couscous, if desired. (The tagine, almonds, and pears can be prepared up to a day

ahead. Cover and refrigerate the stew and pears separately, and reheat over gentle heat before serving. Keep the almonds in an airtight container at room temperature.)

WINE CHÂTEAU PRADEAUX 2000 BANDOL (France, Provence, red) This highly aromatic dish needs a dense, rich wine, and it is worth splurging on this Bandol: its grilled, gamy flavors are accented by dark, brooding fruit notes, and briny hints of roasted herbs.

COURGETTES RONDES FARCIES AU BOULGOUR

Bulgur-Stuffed Round Zucchini

When I first spotted ball-shaped zucchini at the produce stall, they immediately struck me as one of the better horticultural inventions of mankind. Zucchini is a good candidate for stuffing, but the long shape of classic specimens can make them awkward to serve as you lift them from the dish and try to keep the filling in place. Round zucchini, on the other hand, seems to have been created precisely to address this issue: you just slice the hat off — optionally working your knife in zigzags for an eye-catching presentation — carve the inside with a melon baller, *et voilà!* You have the perfect vessel to hold the filling of your choice.

ROUND ZUCCHINI are also called eight-ball zucchini or globe squash. Look for firm, smooth, and shiny ones with no scratches or bruises. Once carved, round zucchini can also be used as serving cups for chilled summer soups, such as gazpacho, or salads, such as Lebanese tabbouleh. ❧

I sometimes make stuffing with meat, but my preference goes to grain-based versions, flavored with spices, nuts, and herbs. They give a moister texture to the ensemble, and I find them a more respectful complement to the discreet taste of zucchini.

1. Preheat the oven to 400°F and grease a medium baking dish with olive oil.

2. Rinse and dry the zucchini. Use a paring knife to cut a neat hat off the top of each. Carve the inside with a melon baller or a sharp-edged spoon, making sure you don't break through the skin. Reserve the flesh. (If you use long zucchini, slice them in two lengthwise, and carve the center to form boat-shaped containers.)

3. Put the zucchini shells and hats in the prepared dish, drizzle with the tablespoon of olive oil, and sprinkle with salt and pepper. Bake for 20 to 25 minutes, until tender but still holding their shape. (This yields tastier results than boiling the shells: it will concentrate and caramelize the flavor of the zucchini.)

4. Meanwhile, cook the bulgur in stock or water according to package instructions and let cool. Toast the pine nuts in a dry skillet.

5. Heat the teaspoon of olive oil in a large skillet over medium-high heat. Add the onions and cook for 5 minutes, stirring regularly, until softened. Add the reserved zucchini flesh and season with salt and pepper. Cover and cook for 5 minutes, stirring from time to time. Remove the lid and cook for 5 more minutes, until all the juices have evaporated. Remove from heat and let cool slightly.

6. When the zucchini shells are tender, take them out of the oven (leave the heat on) and put them upside down on a plate lined with paper towels. Combine the zucchini mixture, bulgur, cinnamon, red pepper flakes, if using, goat cheese, mint, and pine nuts in a medium mixing bowl. Mix thoroughly with a fork. Taste and adjust the seasoning.

7. Set the shells upright in the gratin dish, spoon in the filling, distributing it evenly, and top each zucchini with its hat. (The recipe can be made up to a day ahead up to this point.) Bake for 10 to 15 minutes, until the filling is heated through, and serve immediately.

1 tablespoon plus 1 teaspoon extra virgin olive oil, plus 1 teaspoon for greasing the baking dish

8 round zucchini, about 3 pounds (or 3 pounds of long zucchini)

Fine sea salt and freshly ground pepper

1 cup medium-grind bulgur (pre-cooked and ground wheat berries, available from natural foods stores and Middle Eastern markets)

$1/4$ cup pine nuts

2 medium yellow onions, thinly sliced

$1/2$ teaspoon ground cinnamon

$1/4$ teaspoon red pepper flakes (optional)

2 ounces semidry goat cheese, crumbled

$1/4$ cup (packed) mint leaves, finely chopped

Serves 4 as a light main course

Courgettes Rondes Farcies au Boulgour
Bulgur-Stuffed Round Zucchini, page 128

VARIATIONS Use other grains (barley, quinoa, rice), seasonings (basil, thyme, cumin, curry), nuts (walnuts, cashews), and cheeses (a mild blue cheese, a hard grated cheese). Or, instead of nuts and cheese, try diced tomatoes and pancetta or bacon, diced and sautéed until crisp.

*W*INE FRÉDÉRIC MABILEAU SAINT NICOLAS DE BOURGUEIL LES ROUILLÈRES 2004 (France, Loire, red) Cabernet Franc is a particularly food-friendly varietal. This Bourgueil has a highly aromatic nose of blackberry, black pepper, and spring herbs, which complements the zucchini nicely. It has a low tannin content and an appetite-whetting effect.

BŒUF BOURGUIGNON

Beef Bourguignon

*B*eef Bourguignon is the epitome of the soul-warming, convivial dish that chilly winter nights call for: rich aromas, fork-tender meat, and a smooth sauce that's just screaming to be mopped up with some fresh, crusty bread.

There are three secrets to making a killer beef bourguignon. First, don't skimp on the wine: choose a good bottle of dry red, preferably from Burgundy. Second, the meat and vegetables should be left to marinate overnight in that good wine you bought, to fully absorb its flavors. Finally, a hint of sweetness is needed to balance the acidity in the sauce. Some cooks add brown sugar, some a light caramel. Me, I like to add a little chocolate.

1. Start the marinade 12 hours or up to a day in advance. Combine the onion, shallots, carrots, garlic, thyme, parsley, and bay leaves in a large mixing bowl. Season generously with salt and pepper, add the olive oil, and toss to coat. Add the beef and toss again. Pour in the wine, cover with plastic wrap, and refrigerate for 12 hours, or up to a day.

1 medium yellow onion, minced

2 medium shallots, minced

3 medium carrots, cut in $^1/_2$-inch slices

2 garlic cloves, minced

2 teaspoons fresh thyme or 1 teaspoon dried thyme

$^1/_4$ cup (packed) fresh flat-leaf parsley leaves, roughly chopped

2 bay leaves

Fine sea salt and freshly ground pepper

2 tablespoons extra virgin olive oil

$3^1/_2$ pounds well-trimmed boneless beef chuck, cut in 2-inch cubes

1 bottle (3 cups) medium-bodied dry red wine, preferably from Burgundy (Mercurey, Côte de Nuits Village, Passetoutgrain), or a good Pinot Noir from California

6 ounces thickly sliced uncooked bacon, cut in $^1/_2$-inch strips

3 tablespoons all-purpose flour

$1^1/_2$ ounces semisweet chocolate, broken into bits

Small steamed potatoes or cooked pasta for serving

---— ❋ —---

Serves 6 as a main course
Marinating time: 12 hours

2. When you're ready to cook the stew, pour the marinade, meat, and vegetables through a colander into a second large bowl, to save the liquids and solids separately. Remove the meat from the colander (it doesn't matter if a few bits of vegetables stick to the meat), and set aside on a plate.

3. Set a large heavy pot or Dutch oven over medium-high heat, add the bacon, and cook until crisp. Remove the bacon with a slotted spoon and set aside. If there is more than 2 tablespoons of bacon drippings in the pan, pour out the excess fat.

4. Add the marinated vegetables and cook for 5 minutes, until softened, stirring regularly. Remove the vegetables from the pan and return to the bowl.

5. Working in two batches, place the meat in a single layer in the pan without crowding and cook until browned on all sides, about 8 minutes per batch. When the second batch is done, return the first batch to the pot, sprinkle with flour, and toss until no white trace of flour remains. Add the vegetables, pour in the reserved marinade, and stir. Bring to a simmer, turn the heat down to low, cover, and cook for 3 hours. About 1 hour into the cooking, add the chocolate and reserved bacon.

6. Remove the lid, turn the heat up to medium-high, and cook for 20 minutes, stirring regularly, until the sauce is thick enough to cling to the meat. Transfer to a serving dish or serve straight from the pot, with small steamed potatoes or pasta (fish out the bay leaves before serving, or simply tell your dining companions not to eat them). A bit of bread is also welcome to mop up the sauce.

Bœuf Bourguignon
Beef Bourguignon

NOTE For deeper flavors, it is best to cook Beef Bourguignon a day ahead. Start the marinade two days in advance. Cook the stew the next day, cool uncovered on the counter, cover, and refrigerate. On the third and final day, skim the fat from the surface, reheat over gentle heat, and serve.

*W*INE Serve the same wine as was used in the stew.

CARBONADES FLAMANDES

Flemish Carbonades

My father's side of the family is originally from the French Flanders in the north of France. Most of us live in other parts of the country now and I had never set foot there until one summer a few years ago, when a work project sent me to Lille.

Apart from the whole getting-up-at-dawn-to-catch-the-six-A.M.-train thing, I happen to love business trips: I see them as a unique occasion to be on my own in an unfamiliar city, spread my mess around a hotel room, treat myself to dinner, and pretend I'm a character in a novel. And in this instance, I was even happier for the opportunity to spend time in the land of my forebears.

As I always do before I travel, I conducted a little research to know which local dishes shouldn't be missed. Waffles and *potjevleesch* (a three-meat terrine) sounded good, but I was particularly eager to try the Flemish *carbonades*, a beef stew made with beer, which can be described as the northern beef Bourguignon since beer is to Flanders what red wine is to Burgundy.

I ordered it one night at a small restaurant, and it was brought to my table in a cast-iron pot, with a hefty side of golden fries. The whole thing disappeared into my stomach (I did stop at the cast-iron pot) and as soon as I'd recovered my senses, I added this beautiful dish to my must-cook list.

In addition to beef and beer, carbonades involve onions, brown sugar, and, as a clever trick to add body and balance to the sauce, two slices of day-old bread, spread with strong mustard. It is a truly enthralling stew that leaves the guests in a state of smiling contentment, wiping the last drops of sauce and murmuring their assent.

1. Melt the butter over medium heat in a large heavy pot or Dutch oven. Add half of the meat in a single layer and cook for 3 to 4 minutes on each side, until browned. Transfer to a plate and brown the remaining pieces. Return all the meat to the pot, sprinkle with salt, pepper, and flour, and stir to coat. Add the onions and stir; the pot will seem quite full. Cook for 5 minutes, stirring regularly to avoid coloring.

2. Pour in 1 cup warm water and scrape the bottom of the pot with a wooden spoon to dissolve the caramelized juices (this is called deglazing). Pour in the beer and an additional cup of water, stir, and bring to a simmer.

3. Add the sugar, thyme, bay leaves, and cloves, and stir. Lower the heat to medium-low, cover, and simmer for 2½ hours, stirring every once in a while. An hour into the cooking, spread each slice of bread with a tablespoon of mustard and place at the surface of the stew. The bread will soon be moistened by the steam inside the pot and will fall apart as you stir, giving body to the sauce.

4. Remove the lid, turn the heat up to medium-high, and cook for 20 more minutes, stirring regularly, until the sauce is thick enough to cling to the meat. Serve hot from the pot (fish out the bay leaves before serving, or simply warn your dining companions not to eat them; don't worry about the cloves, they dissolve magically in the stew), with small steamed potatoes.

NOTE For deeper flavors, it is best to make the carbonades a day ahead. Once the stew is cooked, cool uncovered on the counter, cover, and refrigerate. The next day, skim the fat from the surface, reheat over gentle heat, and serve.

VARIATION An alternate version of this recipe calls for *Pain d'Épice* (see page 175) instead of bread and mustard: add 2 tablespoons red wine vinegar as you deglaze the pan, omit the sugar, and use 4 ounces Pain d'Épice (about three ⅓-inch slices) when the recipe instructs you to add the bread slices.

*ℬ*EER Serve the same beer as was used in the stew.

2 tablespoons unsalted butter

3½ pounds well-trimmed boneless beef chuck, cut in 1-inch slices

½ teaspoon fine sea salt

¼ teaspoon freshly ground pepper

3 tablespoons all-purpose flour

2 pounds yellow onions, about 6 medium, sliced

3 cups (24 fluid ounces, usually 2 bottles) rich amber ale — a French *bière de garde,* a *gueuze* from Brussels, or a good ale from a micro-brewery near you

3 tablespoons light brown sugar

1 tablespoon fresh thyme or 1½ teaspoons dried thyme

2 bay leaves

3 whole cloves

Two ½-inch-thick slices day-old peasant-style bread (not sourdough), about 2 ounces each

2 tablespoons strong Dijon mustard

❈

Serves 6 as a main course

Accompagnements

SIDES

Ratatouille au Four

ROASTED RATATOUILLE

Courgettes aux Olives

ZUCCHINI WITH OLIVES

Fenouil Braisé au Romarin

ROSEMARY BRAISED FENNEL

Purée aux Anchois

MASHED POTATOES WITH ANCHOVIES

Triangles de Polenta Croustillante

CRISP POLENTA TRIANGLES

RATATOUILLE AU FOUR

Roasted Ratatouille

*B*oth my mother and my grandmother make a stupendous ratatouille, but apparently it is a gene I failed to inherit. After cooking too many ratatouilles that were bitter, watery, mushy, or all of the above, I decided to branch out from the stovetop method and fire up my good friend the oven.

This roasted approach is not very traditional — I can sense generations of Provençal cooks shaking their fists in my general direction — but it needs less baby-sitting than the classic technique: you simply combine the vegetables with olive oil and herbs, then forget them for a while in the oven as you go check your e-mail. And by the time you remember to look in on them, they're all roasted and caramelized.

Ratatouille can be served cold or at room temperature as a first course or light lunch (I top it with a poached egg and let the yolk meld with the syrupy juices), or warm, as a side to fish, poultry, or an herb-crusted roast. It is best made in the summer when the vegetables are at their peak, and it will taste noticeably better if you prepare it a day ahead.

2 medium yellow onions, sliced

2 garlic cloves, minced

1 medium eggplant, cut in $^1/_2$-inch slices

3 small zucchini, cut in $^1/_2$-inch slices

2 medium bell peppers, one yellow, one red, cut in strips

8 medium tomatoes, preferably Roma or vine-ripened tomatoes, cut in $^1/_2$-inch slices

1 tablespoon fresh rosemary leaves or $1^1/_2$ teaspoons dried rosemary

1 tablespoon fresh thyme leaves or $1^1/_2$ teaspoons dried thyme

$^1/_2$ teaspoon fine sea salt

Extra virgin olive oil

Freshly ground pepper

Serves 6 as a side

1. Preheat the oven to 350°F. Combine the vegetables and herbs in a large mixing bowl. Season with salt, drizzle with liberal amounts of olive oil, and toss to coat. Transfer into a large baking dish; the dish may seem quite full, but the vegetables will shrink as they bake.

2. Cover the dish tightly with foil and bake for 45 minutes. At this point the vegetables should be softened

but not colored, and there should be cooking juices at the bottom of the dish. Remove the foil and stir. Return to the oven for 30 to 45 minutes, stirring halfway through, until the cooking juices have thickened and the vegetables are slightly browned. Season with freshly ground pepper, taste, and adjust the seasoning.

COURGETTES AUX OLIVES

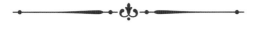
Zucchini with Olives

Zucchini is my little black dress of sides. Most of the time I cook it in such a simple way that I could do it in my sleep, with just a little olive oil, garlic, and herbs. But when I feel like accessorizing it (say, with a scarf or pin), this recipe is a good variation: it introduces black olives for added tang, and a dash of white wine to deepen the flavors. A great side for fish, pork, or roasted chicken, it can also be served as a vegetarian dish over pasta or polenta, with curls of hard cheese, such as Pecorino or aged Comté.

1. Heat the olive oil in a large skillet over medium heat. Add three of the olives (reserve the others) and cook for a minute, until fragrant. Add the onion and garlic and cook for 4 minutes, until softened, stirring regularly to avoid coloring. Add the zucchini, sprinkle with salt, pepper, and herbes de Provence, and stir to combine. Cover and cook for 5 minutes.

2. Add the white wine and the reserved olives, and stir again. Turn the heat to medium-high and cook, uncovered, for 5 to 7 minutes, until most of the juices have evaporated. Serve hot, at room temperature, or cold.

1¹⁄₂ teaspoons extra virgin olive oil

12 black Greek olives, such as Kalamata, pitted and chopped

1 large onion, thinly sliced

2 garlic cloves, minced

1¹⁄₂ pounds zucchini, trimmed and thinly sliced

Fine sea salt and freshly ground pepper

1 teaspoon herbes de Provence (or a mix of dried rosemary, basil, oregano, and thyme)

¹⁄₃ cup dry white wine

Serves 4 as a side

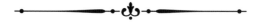

FENOUIL BRAISÉ AU ROMARIN

Rosemary Braised Fennel

*M*y feelings about fennel are strangely ambivalent. I have a screaming dislike for anything aniseed, so I avoid raw fennel like the plague. But if you take that same vegetable, caramelize it in olive oil, and cook it tenderly in a flavorful broth (a process called braising), I will go weak in the knees and eat plateful upon plateful of the soft, sweet wedges, made even more palatable by a silky coating of acidulated juices.

Braised fennel is a fine accompaniment to fish or poultry, and it reheats very well the next day. It can also be served as a salad, topped with thinly sliced goat cheese.

4 small fennel bulbs, about 2 pounds

1 tablespoon extra virgin olive oil

$^{1}/_{4}$ teaspoon sea salt

1 tablespoon chopped fresh rosemary or
  $1^{1}/_{2}$ teaspoons dried rosemary

$^{1}/_{2}$ cup dry white wine

$^{1}/_{2}$ cup good-quality vegetable or chicken
  stock

1 tablespoon freshly squeezed lime juice

Serves 4 as a side

1. Trim the stalks from the fennel. Discard or reserve for a vegetable stock. Quarter each bulb and carve out the core at the base, leaving just a thin portion of the core so the quarters won't fall apart as they cook.

2. Heat the olive oil in a large skillet over medium-high heat. Working in two batches, add the fennel in a single layer without crowding. Cook for 5 to 7 minutes on each side until golden, shaking the pan from time to time. Set the first batch aside on a plate, add a little more olive oil to the pan, and brown the other batch. Return all fennel pieces to the pan.

3. Sprinkle with salt and rosemary. Add the wine, stock, and lime juice. Bring to a simmer and cover. Turn the heat to medium-low and cook for 20 to 25 minutes, until tender. Remove the lid, turn the heat up to medium-high, and cook for 5 minutes, until the juices are syrupy. Serve warm, at room temperature, or cold.

VARIATION Use $^{1}/_{2}$ teaspoon orange zest and 2 tablespoons orange juice instead of lime.

PURÉE AUX ANCHOIS

Mashed Potatoes with Anchovies

When I was growing up, there was always a box of instant mashed potatoes in the kitchen somewhere. It was usually in the cabinet above the sink, but if it wasn't there you could check the one above the collapsible cutting board. It was called *purée mousseline*, and it was a quick enough dinner with a slice of ham when my parents were out for the evening — *jambon-purée* is the equivalent of mac and cheese on the French comfort food scale. I never quite mastered the art of adding the right amount of milk to the potato flakes, however, and I usually ended up with a very thin potato soup or a mixture so thick it could have been used for bricklaying. I loved it nonetheless.

It was not until my twenties that I first cooked mashed potatoes from scratch and discovered that it was, in fact, less tricky than purée mousseline. Tastier, too, I am told, but my loyalty to this childhood staple prevents me from admitting as much.

Plain mashed potatoes are enchanting just as they are, but I like to spike them up for a change of pace: fresh chives or parsley added at the last minute, a handful of chopped walnuts, slivers of truffles for special occasions, or olive oil and anchovies, as in the recipe below. You can't taste the anchovies as such, but their pungent saltiness lifts the overall flavor. This is a good match to roasted pork or pan-seared fish, and it is heavenly with duck magret.

2 pounds baking potatoes (russet or Yukon gold)

1 teaspoon fine sea salt

8 fillets dry-salted anchovies packed in salt or olive oil, rinsed and patted dry if packed in salt, chopped

2 garlic cloves, finely minced or pressed

1/4 teaspoon freshly ground pepper

1/4 cup extra virgin olive oil

1/2 cup crème fraîche, heavy cream, half-and-half, or milk

Serves 4 to 6 as a side

1. Peel and cut the potatoes in 1/2-inch slices. Rinse under cold water and transfer to a large saucepan. Add cold water to cover the potatoes by an inch and add the salt. Set over medium-high heat, cover, and bring to a simmer. Remove the lid, lower the heat to medium, and cook for 15 to 20 minutes, until tender.

2. While the potatoes cook, mash the anchovies, garlic, pepper, and 1 tablespoon of the olive oil with a mortar and pestle, or with a bowl and fork. Combine the anchovy mixture with the cream and warm up for a few seconds in the microwave (or in a small saucepan over medium heat), until hot but not boiling.

3. Drain the potatoes and return to the pan. Add the anchovy mixture and the remaining 3 tablespoons olive oil. Set the pan over medium-low heat, and mash the potatoes with a fork or potato ricer, incorporating the other ingredients. Taste, adjust the seasoning, and keep warm until ready to serve.

TRIANGLES DE POLENTA CROUSTILLANTE

Crisp Polenta Triangles

Polente is prominently featured in the regional cuisine of Savoie in the French Alps, where it was brought back from Piedmont at the time of its annexation by the Duke of Savoy. And yet good cornmeal is hard to come by elsewhere in France: you need to go to small Italian shops or fine foods stores, where you will be charged an arm and a leg for what was originally peasant food, eaten as a substitute for potatoes and bread when they were scarce.

So whenever friends of mine go skiing in the Alps (I myself love snow and fondues, but I am a bit ski-phobic), I drop king-size hints about how happy a package of stone-ground polenta would make me. And when they do indulge me, I express my gratitude by baking these triangles for them: crisp at the edges and softhearted, they are flavored with Beaufort cheese and walnuts, two other ingredients that Savoie justifiably takes pride in.

Polenta triangles can be served with stews and braised dishes, good sausages (especially if you come across *diots*, those plump Savoyard sausages), or a simple grilled fish. I also serve them as a fast-vanishing finger food or atop a salad.

1. Heat the milk and 2 cups water in a large heavy saucepan over medium heat. Add the salt and pepper. Just before the liquids start to simmer, sprinkle the polenta into the pot slowly while stirring with a whisk. Turn the heat to low and keep whisking the mixture, without letting it boil, until it thickens and pulls away from the sides of the pan. This will take about 5 minutes if you use quick cooking, 30 minutes if you use stone ground — in the latter case, after the first 5 minutes, you don't need to whisk it constantly, just regularly, to keep it from burning. (Be careful: as the polenta cooks, the mixture will form burping bubbles that could erupt on your hands.)

2 cups milk

$3/4$ teaspoon fine sea salt

$1/4$ teaspoon freshly ground pepper

1 cup medium-grind polenta, stone-ground or quick-cooking

1 tablespoon extra virgin olive oil, plus 2 teaspoons for greasing

1 teaspoon herbes de Provence (or a mix of dried rosemary, basil, oregano, and thyme)

$1/2$ cup walnuts, lightly toasted and chopped

1 cup freshly grated Beaufort, about $3^1/2$ ounces (substitute Gruyère or Comté)

❋

*Serves 6 as a side,
10 to 12 as an appetizer
Chilling time: 1 hour*

2. Remove from heat, stir in the oil, herbes de Provence, walnuts, and half of the cheese (cover the other half and reserve in the fridge for the topping). Grease a large rectangular baking dish with 1 teaspoon oil and pour in the polenta mixture, spreading it with a spatula. Press plastic wrap directly on the polenta, and refrigerate for an hour or overnight.

3. Preheat the oven to 400°F. Line a baking sheet with foil and grease it with 1 teaspoon oil. Use a sharp knife to cut the polenta into squares about 2 by 2 inches (wipe the knife blade when it gets too coated with polenta), and cut each square diagonally to form triangles. Use a spatula — preferably a thin and narrow one — to transfer the triangles onto the baking sheet, leaving just a little space between them. Sprinkle with the reserved cheese — don't worry if some of the cheese lands on the foil.

4. Bake for 10 to 12 minutes, until the sides of the triangles get lightly crusty. Switch to broiler setting and broil for 5 minutes, until golden, keeping an eye on them. Let cool for a minute, and use the spatula to loosen and lift the triangles from the foil. Serve immediately, or at room temperature.

VARIATIONS You can omit the walnuts, or substitute Parmesan and pine nuts for the Beaufort and walnuts.

Buffet

Mini-Quiches Poulet & Noix de Cajou
CHICKEN AND CASHEW MINI-QUICHES

Mini Croque-Monsieur

Gâteau de Quinoa, Champignons & Bacon
QUINOA, BACON, AND MUSHROOM CAKE

Cake Tomate, Pistache & Chorizo
TOMATO, PISTACHIO, AND CHORIZO LOAF

Terrine de Foies de Volaille aux Figues
CHICKEN LIVER AND FIG TERRINE

Crumble de Courgettes, Figues & Mozzarella
ZUCCHINI CRUMBLE WITH FIGS AND MOZZARELLA

Mousseline de Cabillaud à l'Aubergine
EGGPLANT AND COD TERRINE

*B*irthdays, new apartments, new jobs, and new years are all excellent excuses to throw a party, but you don't really need one at all. Just the sudden impulse to gather your friends for a bit of chatting, eating, drinking, and optionally dancing, if you are fearless of the downstairs neighbors' wrath.

For parties, I prepare two kinds of savory edibles: an assortment of appetizers to welcome our friends as they arrive, and a few larger main dishes, served from a buffet later in the evening, when most of the guests are here.

The menu planning process is similar to that of a seated dinner party (see page 113), but here you want to focus on dishes that can be prepared ahead of time and enjoyed warm or at room temperature; dishes that can be easily shared and eaten with just a fork, while standing up, and without embarrassing oneself with stubborn pieces of meat or juices that squirt and dribble down one's chin.

I don't recommend super-sizing your favorite recipes, unless you are certain they will scale up well. Most of the time they don't — there isn't enough dressing to go around, or the seasoning is overzealous — and I prefer to cook several regular-size dishes, knowing that people will enjoy the variety and have a small serving of each.

A cheese platter is a crowd-pleasing dish that is quick to assemble and feeds many. People often make a mess of it, happily ignoring the proper cutting rules, but it's fun to watch. Pick four or five different kinds, and avoid the ones that have a pungent aroma — washed-rind cheeses in particular — or the whole room will smell like a gym. And if you decide to serve a cheese platter, make sure you buy plenty of bread (serve it with crackers if you must, but it is a rather un-French thing to do).

As for the dessert selection, it should offer options to suit everyone's tastes: something fiercely chocolaty for the likes of me, but also something fresh and fruity, such as a tart, a crumble, or a simple fruit basket — choose varieties that can be eaten tidily out of hand. Cookies couldn't be easier to serve — no slicing necessary — and they're usually the first things to disappear.

If you have friends who cook and you could use a bit of help (in my experience, one can always use a bit of help), see if they wouldn't mind bringing something. Trying your best not to sound bossy or demanding or both, make sure it will be a dish that can be set straight on the table, after a bit of reheating at the most, and suggest the kind of preparation that will round your menu nicely — a salad, a quiche, a cake, etc.

The recipes in this section are all fit for a buffet. Naturally, they could just as well be served under other circumstances, for a weeknight meal or a dinner party.

MINI-QUICHES POULET & NOIX DE CAJOU

Chicken and Cashew Mini-Quiches

$\mathcal{T}$hese miniature crustless quiches make appealing handheld bites, which will be nibbled on or wolfed down, depending on the eater. Filled with strips of chicken, diced tomatoes, and crunchy cashews, they are baked until golden and lightly crusty but still nice and moist inside. Mini-quiches are good soldiers for a buffet: they can be eaten warm or at room temperature, and you can bake them up to a day ahead (reheat for ten minutes in a warm oven before serving).

1. Heat the olive oil in a small skillet over medium heat. Add the garlic and cook for a few seconds, until fragrant. Add the chicken, if raw, and season with $^{1}/_{4}$ teaspoon of the salt and $^{1}/_{4}$ teaspoon of the pepper. Cover and cook for 3 to 4 minutes on each side, until golden and cooked through, but not tough. Let cool and cut in $^{1}/_{2}$-inch pieces. Halve and core the tomatoes, discard the juice and seeds, and dice the flesh.

2. Whisk the eggs in a large mixing bowl. Add the milk and whisk again. Sift in the flour, season with the remaining $^{1}/_{2}$ teaspoon salt and $^{1}/_{4}$ teaspoon pepper, and whisk until blended — the batter will be thin. Add the chicken, cheese, tomatoes, tarragon, and cashews. Stir with a spoon to blend. (The batter can be made a day ahead, covered, and refrigerated. Give it a good stir before using the next day.)

3. Preheat the oven to 425°F and grease a mini or regular-size muffin tin with olive oil.

1 teaspoon extra virgin olive oil, plus extra for greasing

1 garlic clove, minced

6 ounces boneless, skinless free-range chicken breast meat, uncooked, or 1 cup (packed) cooked chicken strips

$^{3}/_{4}$ teaspoon fine sea salt

$^{1}/_{2}$ teaspoon freshly ground pepper

4 Roma or plum tomatoes, about 12 ounces

3 large eggs

$1^{1}/_{2}$ cups milk

$^{3}/_{4}$ cup whole wheat (or all-purpose) flour

1 cup freshly grated Gruyère or Comté, about $3^{1}/_{2}$ ounces

2 tablespoons (packed) chopped fresh tarragon leaves (substitute fresh flat-leaf parsley or cilantro leaves)

$^{2}/_{3}$ cup cashews, toasted and roughly chopped (see page 6)

Makes 12 medium or 24 mini-quiches

4. Spoon the batter evenly into the prepared muffin tin and bake for 25 to 35 minutes, depending on the size of your molds, until golden and puffy. Transfer to a rack to cool for 2 minutes. Unmold, let cool for 10 minutes, and serve warm or at room temperature.

VARIATION In the fall and winter, you can make a mushroom version of these quiches: substitute parsley for the tarragon and 9 ounces fresh cremini mushrooms for the tomatoes (3 cups when trimmed and chopped; add them raw to the batter).

*W*INE DOMAINE DE LA MADONE 2004 BEAUJOLAIS-VILLAGES (France, Beaujolais, red) Beaujolais works particularly well on chicken and tomato combinations. This one displays fruity notes of cherry, raspberry, and violet, with a nice acidity and a light texture. Pinot Grigio and other light, crisp wines will work well, too.

MINI CROQUE-MONSIEUR

*C*roque-monsieur is the French grilled cheese sandwich, made with Gruyère and brine-cured ham on white sandwich bread. Most Parisian brasseries drench it with a rich béchamel sauce; I prefer it homemade and sans béchamel.

When my mother made croque-monsieur I liked to act as her assistant, helping her butter the bread and crank the cheese through our bright orange rotary grater. She would then grill the sandwiches on the stove, using an old-fashioned iron that imprinted the shape of a scallop shell on the bread.

BRINE-CURED HAM is a ham that is soaked in, or injected with brine, then boiled or smoked, and sometimes aged. Such hams, also called city hams, are usually light pink; they are moister, milder, and less salty than dry-cured hams.

As a little girl the crust was the part I least enjoyed, so I would eat that first to get it over with, slicing it off neatly until I was left with a golden square of crisp toasted bread and gooey filling. This in turn would be cut into dainty cubes, which I would eat methodically, one by one, maintaining — and this was very important — a symmetrical pattern on my plate.

Croque-monsieur lend themselves well to miniaturization. When I serve bite-size ones at parties they disappear in a heartbeat, and I think a large part of this success can be explained by the fact that I slice off the crusts, so my guests won't have to.

1. Preheat the oven to 400°F and line a baking sheet with foil or parchment paper.

2. Working on a large cutting board, spread the bread slices with butter. Slice off and discard the crusts of the bread (or leave them out to dry for a day and mix in a blender to make bread crumbs). Flip the slices on the cutting board so the buttered sides face down. Divide the cheese among all the slices, top half of the slices with ham, and sprinkle with pepper. Assemble the slices into sandwiches two by two — one with ham, one without — so the exterior faces of each sandwich are buttered. Transfer to the baking sheet.

3. Bake for 10 minutes, until the sandwiches are golden on top. Remove the sheet from the oven (leave the heat on). Transfer the sandwiches to the cutting board and let rest for a few minutes, until cool enough to handle. Use a sharp bread knife to cut each sandwich into nine equal squares if the slices are large, four if they are medium. Flip each of the mini-sandwiches as you put them back on the baking sheet, and bake for another 7 minutes, until golden. Let cool for a few minutes and serve warm or at room temperature.

VARIATIONS Spread a little mustard on the ham once you've arranged it on the cheese. For a quick and felicitous lunch, make a regular-size croque-monsieur and top it with an egg, sunny side up: this is called a *croque-madame*.

*W*INE LABOURE ROI 2004 POUILLY-FUISSÉ (France, Burgundy, white) This buttery and toasty Chardonnay matches the bread and mild cheese flavors of this dish. Despite its oaky accents, it is lightly fruity, with notes of apple and pear. It displays hints of honey and hazelnut, too, and a gentle acidity.

8 large slices good-quality white or multigrain sandwich bread, or 16 medium slices, about 12 ounces

3 tablespoons unsalted butter, at room temperature

1 cup freshly grated Comté or Gruyère, about 3 1/2 ounces

6 ounces thinly sliced brine-cured ham (see page 00), trimmed and cut in bite-size strips

Freshly ground pepper

Makes 32 to 36 pieces, depending on the size of the bread

Mini-Quiches Poulet & Noix de Cajou
Chicken and Cashew Mini-Quiches, page 147

Cake Tomate, Pistache & Chorizo
Tomato, Pistachio, and Chorizo Loaf, page 153

GÂTEAU DE QUINOA, CHAMPIGNONS & BACON

Quinoa, Bacon, and Mushroom Cake

I can spend hours in natural foods stores. The ones in Paris are — as everything seems to be — considerably smaller than their American counterparts, but they are filled with intriguing products that promise to add a twist to my habitual diet.

What inspires me the most is the variety of grains that such stores offer: we are all on a first-name basis with wheat, oat, and rice, but how many can say as much about amaranth and millet, spelt and barley? Besides their health benefits and fascinating history — most have been cultivated for millennia and I find it tickling to eat a grain that was an Incan staple — they truly open up new horizons for the taste buds.

Quinoa in particular is very easy to love: it cooks faster than most grains, and its seeds, unfurling into tiny snails, become both fluffy and crunchy. This savory quinoa cake enhances the nutty flavor of the grain with soft mushrooms and smoky bacon bits. It can be cut in wedges and served as part of a buffet in the fall, or paired with a simple salad for lunch.

2 cups uncooked quinoa, rinsed

6 thick slices bacon, about 6 ounces

1 medium yellow onion, chopped

1 pound cremini mushrooms, stems cut off, brushed clean, and sliced

1 teaspoon oil for greasing pan

3 large eggs

$1/4$ cup heavy cream

$1/2$ teaspoon fine sea salt

$1/2$ teaspoon freshly ground pepper

$1/2$ cup (loosely packed) fresh flat-leaf parsley leaves, chopped

Serves 10 to 12 as a main course or buffet item

1. Cook the quinoa in stock or salted water according to package instructions. Drain and set aside. Cook the bacon in a skillet over medium-high heat, until brown and crisp. Transfer to a plate lined with paper towels. When cooled, crumble it roughly.

2. Pour out the excess fat from the skillet and lower the heat to medium. Add the onion and cook for 8 minutes, until softened, stirring regularly. Add the sliced mushrooms, cover, and cook for 5 minutes, until browned. Remove the lid and cook for 2 minutes, until most of the juices have evaporated.

3. Preheat the oven to 400°F and grease a 10-inch springform cake pan with oil.

4. Whisk the eggs, cream, salt, and pepper in a large mixing bowl. Add the quinoa and mushroom mixture and stir until blended. Fold in the bacon and parsley. Pour into the prepared cake pan, level the surface with a spatula, and bake for 35 minutes, until the top is golden and crusty, and a knife inserted in the center comes out clean.

5. Transfer the pan to a cooling rack and let stand for 5 minutes. Run a knife around the pan to loosen and unclasp the sides of the pan. Cut in square pieces or wedges with a serrated knife and serve warm or at room temperature. The cake can be made a day ahead, tightly wrapped, and refrigerated. Reheat for 10 minutes in a 350°F oven before serving.

VARIATION In late spring and summer, use cubes of goat cheese, diced tomatoes, and basil, instead of the bacon, mushrooms, and parsley.

*W*INE THE FIFTEEN 2000 GRENACHE (France, Languedoc-Roussillon, red) This wine displays earthy aromas of mushrooms and wet soil, with hints of black pepper and smoky spice. The fruit — subdued notes of black cherry — is restrained enough for this dish.

CAKE TOMATE, PISTACHE & CHORIZO

Tomato, Pistachio, and Chorizo Loaf

*T*he English word "cake" is used in French for a variety of baked goods made in a loaf pan. Sweet versions are often flavored with candied fruit (*cake aux fruits confits*) or lemon (*cake au citron*), while savory ones (*cakes salés*) can accommodate all manner of fillings — vegetables, nuts, cheese, dry-cured meat, fish, etc.

Cut in slices or cubes, these savory loaves make frequent appearances on French buffets and picnic spreads, or as a finger food for the apéritif. Truth be told, I often find them much too dry, each bite urgently requiring a gulp of water to wash it down or a Heimlich maneuver if there is no glass within immediate reach.

I myself baked my fair share of less-than-stellar cakes salés, but I couldn't quite let go of the ambition to produce a palatable one. I experimented with many a recipe before I finally understood — "Eureka!" exclaimed the cook in her bathtub — that yogurt was the key to an ideally moist crumb. This version is a favorite, featuring pistachios, sun-dried tomatoes, and chorizo in a flavor-packed *ménage à trois*.

1 tablespoon unsalted butter

2 tablespoons sesame seeds — one for the pan, one for topping

1^1/4 cups all-purpose flour

1 tablespoon baking powder

3 large eggs

^{1}/2 teaspoon fine sea salt

^{1}/2 teaspoon freshly ground pepper

^{1}/4 cup extra virgin olive oil

^{1}/2 cup plain unsweetened yogurt (preferably whole milk), Greek-style yogurt, or buttermilk

3^1/2 ounces Spanish air-dried chorizo, preferably spicy, skin removed if any, and diced (substitute cooked Mexican chorizo or pepperoni)

12 sun-dried tomato halves packed in oil, drained and finely diced

^{3}/4 cup shelled unsalted pistachios, toasted (available from gourmet or natural foods stores, or Middle Eastern markets; if you can only find salted pistachios, see page 80)

^{3}/4 cup (loosely packed) fresh flat-leaf parsley leaves, chopped

Serves 8 to 10 as a starter or buffet item

1. Preheat the oven to 350°F. Butter a 9 by 5-inch loaf pan, sprinkle half of the sesame seeds onto the bottom and sides, and shake the pan to coat.

2. Combine the flour and baking powder in a small mixing bowl and set aside. In a medium mixing bowl, whisk together the eggs, salt, and pepper. Pour in the oil and yogurt, and whisk again. Sift the flour mixture into the egg mixture and stir with a wooden spoon until incorporated. Don't overmix the batter — it's okay if a few lumps remain. Fold in the chorizo, sun-dried tomatoes, pistachios, and parsley. Stir to combine. Pour the batter into the prepared pan, level the surface with a spatula, and sprinkle with the remaining sesame seeds.

3. Bake for 40 to 50 minutes, until the loaf is golden and a knife inserted in the center comes out clean. Let cool for a few minutes on the counter, run a knife around the pan to loosen, unmold, and transfer to a rack to cool completely. Cut in slices or cubes just before serving. (The loaf can be made up to a day ahead, wrapped tightly in foil, and refrigerated. Bring to room temperature before serving.)

VARIATIONS Use dried figs or dates instead of sun-dried tomatoes. The same batter (from flour to yogurt) can be used with infinite combinations of ingredients: nuts and herbs, olives, cut up sautéed or roasted vegetables, strips of ham or chicken, cubes of cheese, fresh fruit, etc.

*W*INE MONTECILLO 2001 RIOJA CRIANZA (Spain, Rioja, red) This wine has a nose of black cherry, peppery spice, and leather. The palate offers similar notes, with balanced flavors of cherry and fig. It is medium-bodied and tannic, with an acidity that responds well to the tomatoes.

TERRINE DE FOIES DE VOLAILLE AUX FIGUES

Chicken Liver and Fig Terrine

*B*eyond the bold gaminess of their flavors, what I love about meat terrines is that the recipes were often created to use up lesser cuts of meat, making them gloriously thrifty dishes, and a haven for underappreciated bits and pieces.

It is rare for city cooks to prepare meat terrines at home — they are so readily available from charcuteries, why would one bother — and many of them call for puzzling animal ingredients (calves' hooves, pork back fat, or even caul, the lacy membrane taken from the abdomen of a cow or sheep), the kind you have to request from your butcher tentatively, hoping he at least will know what you're talking about.

But this smooth terrine is quite simple to shop for: it uses whole chicken livers (they can be purchased fresh from the butcher's if you have access to one, or at the grocery store short of that), whose unabashedly earthy character is softened by port and plump morsels of dried figs. Served with thickly sliced toasts of crusty bread, it is a rustic-chic dish that will do well as a starter, or as part of a buffet. It is best made a day ahead, so the texture will set and the flavors will have time to develop.

1. Rinse the livers under cold water, drain, and remove any white strands. Pat dry with paper towels. Combine the livers and port in a small salad bowl. Cover and refrigerate for 2 hours. Set a fine-mesh sieve over a second bowl and pour the livers and marinade into the sieve, reserving the marinade.

1 pound fresh chicken livers

1/2 cup port wine

8 dried black Mission figs

8 tablespoons (1 stick) unsalted butter, diced

2 small shallots, minced

1 garlic clove, minced

1 teaspoon fresh thyme or 1/2 teaspoon dried thyme

2 bay leaves

1/2 teaspoon fine sea salt

1/4 teaspoon freshly ground pepper

Serves 12 to 16 as a starter or buffet item (the recipe can be halved)
Chilling time: 2 hours for the marinade, 6 hours for the finished terrine

2. Wash the first bowl you used. Put the figs in the bowl, cover with hot water, and let stand as you go on with the recipe.

3. Melt 2 tablespoons of the butter in a large skillet over medium heat. Add the shallots and garlic and cook for 3 minutes, until softened and fragrant. Add the livers, thyme, bay leaves, salt, and pepper, and cook for 4 minutes, flipping the livers halfway through, until the livers are browned on the outside, but still pink inside. Add the reserved marinade, turn the heat up to medium-high, and cook for 6 to 8 minutes, until most of the liquids have evaporated and the livers are browned all over but still tender. Remove from heat, discard the bay leaves, and let cool for 5 minutes.

4. Transfer the liver mixture to a food processor and process until puréed. Add the remaining butter and pulse until smooth. Drain the figs, pat dry with paper towels, cut in 1/4-inch pieces, and fold into the liver mixture. Taste and adjust the seasoning.

5. Pack into two 1-cup glass jars, making sure there are no pockets of air. Place a small piece of plastic wrap directly on the surface of the terrine, close the jars tightly, and refrigerate for at least 6 hours, and preferably overnight.

6. Bring to just under room temperature and serve. The terrine will keep for up to 4 days, chilled, its surface covered with plastic wrap.

VARIATIONS The terrine can be made with other dried fruits, especially prunes and apricots. You can include walnuts or hazelnuts in addition to, or instead of, fruit. For a chunkier texture, reserve a few of the cooked livers before you purée the mixture: chop them roughly, and fold them in as you add the fruits or nuts.

Terrine de Foies de Volaille aux Figues
Chicken Liver and Fig Terrine

*W*INE PIPER HEIDSIECK NV BRUT CUVÉE (France, Champagne, sparkling white) This Champagne is nicely complex, with a mineral, citrusy, and lightly yeasty nose. It is ripe on the palate, rich, but fresh enough to cut through the richness of the terrine. It is intensely bubbly, with apple flavors that respond to the figs.

CRUMBLE DE COURGETTES, FIGUES & MOZZARELLA

Zucchini Crumble with Figs and Mozzarella

*A*lways on the lookout for new ways to feature my beloved zucchini, I was once inspired to pair it with the sweetness of fresh figs and the milkiness of mozzarella. What was initially a fortuitous find — these were simply ingredients I had on hand that day and their harmonious colors augured a good match — became a cherished trio.

It is equally successful in grilled sandwiches, salads, and savory tarts, or in this crumble: the mozzarella and figs form a soft blanket over thick zucchini slices, and the crunchy topping brings out their combined flavors with a salty tang. Serve as a buffet item or main course in late spring or early fall, when figs are honey-sweet and bountiful.

2 teaspoons extra virgin olive oil

1 garlic clove, minced

2 pounds zucchini, trimmed and sliced in $^1/_4$-inch rounds

Fine sea salt and freshly ground pepper

$^3/_4$ cup dried bread crumbs

3 tablespoons chilled unsalted butter, diced

$^1/_2$ cup freshly grated Parmesan, about 2 ounces

2 teaspoons fresh thyme or 1 teaspoon dried thyme

9 ounces mozzarella, preferably buffalo mozzarella

6 ripe medium black Mission figs, trimmed and cut in sixths

Serves 4 as a main course, 6 to 8 as a starter or buffet item

1. Heat the olive oil in a large skillet over medium-high heat. Add the garlic and cook for a few seconds, until fragrant. Add the zucchini and season with salt and pepper. Cover, lower the heat to medium, and cook for 6 minutes, until slightly softened. Remove the lid and cook for another 5 to 6 minutes, stirring gently from time to time, until the rounds are tender but still retain their shape, and most of the juices have evaporated.

2. While the zucchini is cooking, combine the bread crumbs, butter, Parmesan, and thyme in a medium mixing bowl. Rub with the tips of your fingers until the mixture resembles coarse meal. (The zucchini and the crumble mixture can be prepared up to a day ahead and refrigerated in separate airtight containers.)

3. Preheat the oven to 400°F. Arrange the zucchini over the bottom of a large baking dish. Thinly slice the mozzarella and pat dry with paper towels. Arrange the cheese and figs over the zucchini. Sprinkle the crumble mixture over the dish and bake for 20 minutes, until heated through and golden. Serve warm or at room temperature.

*W*INE MARQUIS DE CHASSE 2003 BORDEAUX BLANC RÉSERVE (France, Bordeaux, white) In this blend, the Sauvignon Blanc brings citrusy, grassy notes that complement the zucchini, while the Semillion provides a rich mouthfeel and flavors that hint at fig.

BREAD CRUMBS *To make your own bread crumbs, slice the leftovers from a loaf of country-style bread. Leave on the counter to dry completely for a day or two, or put on a baking sheet in a 200°F oven for 20 minutes or until dry, flipping the slices halfway through. Let cool, grind in a food processor, and transfer to an airtight container. Keep at room temperature for up to 2 months, or freeze.* ❀

MOUSSELINE DE CABILLAUD À L'AUBERGINE

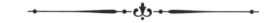

Eggplant and Cod Terrine

I was introduced to fish mousseline — a fluffy fish terrine — at a weekly evening class I took one year to learn about traditional French cooking: since the bulk of my culinary knowledge comes from observing my mother or teaching myself, I had found that some of the more classic French techniques were missing from my arsenal, indispensable things such as aspics, *sauce Mornay*, or the proper way to fry calf's brains.

This class was like hopping aboard a time machine, taking me back to the chubby days of French cuisine, when everything started with an enthusiastic half-pound of butter, when diamond patterns of carrots and leeks were the height of elegance, and when cups of cream were added to soups to, you know, lighten them up.

It was fun, it was fascinating, and I was delighted to work on these old-school dishes with such deliciously quaint names (poached egg *toupinelle, duchesse* potatoes,

1 pound skinless cod fillets, thawed if frozen

$1/4$ teaspoon fine sea salt

$1/2$ teaspoon red pepper flakes

2 large egg whites

1 cup eggplant caviar, homemade (page 77) or store-bought (available from natural or gourmet foods stores and Middle Eastern markets, sometimes marketed as *baba ghanoush*)

$1/3$ cup (loosely packed) fresh flat-leaf parsley leaves, roughly chopped, plus a few stems for garnish

FOR THE BELL PEPPER COULIS

One 14-ounce jar roasted red bell peppers, packed in water, or 2 pounds bell peppers, home-roasted (see page 40)

2 tablespoons extra virgin olive oil

1 garlic clove, peeled, green sprout removed if any

❋

Serves 10 as a starter or buffet item

or *omelette norvégienne*, a dessert that is neither Norwegian nor an omelet), even if we students had to admit that they didn't hold much appeal for our modern-day palates.

But learning the moves of classic French cooking is a bit like studying Latin: the goal is not to actually speak it — at least not on a daily basis — but to better understand the roots and grammar of the languages that derive from it. And indeed, I picked up countless tips and sleights of hand. There was also much inspiration to be milked from these preparations, and I soon noticed that they had a tendency to sneak their way into my daily cooking, after a bit of adjustment to suit my tastes.

This cod terrine is the product of such tweaking. The traditional mousseline is made with fish and cream, but I adapted the recipe to replace the cream with eggplant caviar, a Middle Eastern dip of roasted eggplant. The resulting dish boasts the same mousselike texture as the original, but the substitution adds a bright layer of flavor. I make my own eggplant caviar if I have time, or use a quality store-bought version if I don't. I serve the terrine in slices, with bell pepper coulis on the side: it is an easy-to-make and beautiful complement, both in terms of taste and color.

1. Preheat the oven to 350°F, and line a 9 by 5-inch loaf pan with parchment paper.

2. Remove any bones from the fish with tweezers and cut the fillets in $1/2$-inch pieces. Combine the fish, salt, and red pepper flakes in a food processor and process until finely puréed, working in short pulses. Add the egg whites and eggplant caviar and process until combined. Fold in the chopped parsley. Pour the mixture into the prepared loaf pan, making sure there are no pockets of air, and smooth out the surface with a spatula. Clean the bowl of your food processor thoroughly.

3. Set the loaf pan in a large baking dish and pour hot water into the dish so the bottom of the loaf pan is covered by an inch. Bake for 35 minutes, until the top of the mousseline is set.

4. While the mousseline is baking, prepare the coulis. Drain and seed the bell peppers and combine with the olive oil and garlic in the (cleaned) bowl of your food processor. Process until smooth and transfer into a small jug or serving cup.

5. Set a cooling rack over a plate. Remove the dish and pan from the oven. Lift the mousseline from the loaf pan by pulling cautiously on the parchment paper, and transfer onto the rack. If cooking juices leak from the loaf (this will or won't happen, depending on the eggplant caviar that you used), cut a few slits in the parchment paper at the base of the mousseline so the juices will drain down into the plate.

6. Let cool until slightly warm, or at room temperature. Cut in slices, garnish with parsley, and serve with the bell pepper coulis. (The mousseline and coulis can be made up to a day ahead: wrap the cooled mousseline tightly in foil, cover the coulis with plastic wrap, and refrigerate. Bring to room temperature before serving.)

*W*INE 2004 DOMAINE D'ÉLISE PETIT CHABLIS (France, Burgundy, white) A fish terrine calls for a crisp and delicate wine, and this Petit Chablis is just that: it offers fresh Granny Smith apple aromas, with a slightly tart lemon flavor and mineral notes.

Gourmandise

SWEET THINGS

My mother has always been a prolific baker, and my earliest kitchen memories involve assisting her in the measuring, the pouring, and the stirring of various cake batter ingredients. So it is through the baking door that I first came into the kitchen, and as soon as I had an oven to call my own, I excitedly commandeered it for sweet preparations: although I have no statistics to back this up, it is safe to say that this oven saw many more cakes than it did vegetable gratins.

There is something uniquely fascinating about baking: how the same basic set of ingredients — eggs, butter, sugar, flour — can be turned into such a variety of confections, and how this timeless chemistry goes on behind closed (oven) doors. Something uniquely satisfying, too, since baking is purely pleasure oriented: when you decide to whip up a batch of cookies, it is rarely because you feel your body is in need of the vitamin A that can be found in butter.

My mother's baking always had the elegance of simple things, revolving around French home classics — *quatre-quarts* (the French pound cake), fruit tarts, charlottes, *crème renversée* (an upside-down caramel custard), floating islands — and the occasional incursion into British territory. She would bake a light dessert for dinner perhaps once a week, a cake or some *sablés* to have with tea in the afternoon, and a fruit tart for Sunday lunch. I myself don't bake quite as often — I don't have two growing daughters to feed — but I always jump at the opportunity to do so on special occasions and when we have company.

Gâteaux

CAKES

Gâteau Chocolat & Courgette
CHOCOLATE & ZUCCHINI CAKE

Gâteau Chocolat Framboise
CHOCOLATE RASPBERRY CAKE

Gâteau Ricotta, Abricot & Pistache
APRICOT AND PISTACHIO RICOTTA CAKE

Le Gâteau de Mamy
MY GRANDMOTHER'S APPLE CAKE

Pain d'Épice
HONEY SPICE LOAF

Gâteau au Yaourt
YOGURT CAKE

GÂTEAU CHOCOLAT & COURGETTE
Chocolate & Zucchini Cake

*T*he name for my blog came to me on a bus as I was riding across Paris from my office to my parents' house, where I was expected for dinner. Looking out the window with a notebook on my lap, I was trying to think of something that would have a nice ring to it and would somehow represent me, and my appetite. After a page or two of ideas — some of them quite lame, I must say — *Chocolate & Zucchini* appeared, and it felt instantly right and comfortable, like a favorite pair of jeans.

A fitting name it was, but I didn't at all stop to think whether both ingredients could find their place in the same recipe. When I discovered later that it was common in some parts of the world to use an overflow of garden zucchini in baked goods, it seemed urgent — and a matter of personal honor, really — to add a Chocolate & Zucchini Cake to my repertoire.

To zucchini cake virgins, the combination sounds a little odd — I get a fair amount of raised eyebrows, and the occasional wrinkled nose — but it is surprisingly successful, and there is real teamwork at play: the zucchini makes the crumb moist and fluffy, while the chocolate does its thing and brings deep flavor to the cake. In fact, you could serve it without telling anyone that there is zucchini in it; they would never know and it would be our little secret. But I find it much more entertaining to disclose this key ingredient upfront and watch the puzzled expression on my friends' faces turn into one of delight and wonder, as if they were chewing on some sort of a magic trick. "Zucchini, really?" A pause, and then, "May I have another slice?"

Depending on my mood, the weather, and the alignment of the stars, I make this cake with either butter or olive oil: butter gives it a round richness, but olive oil slips in an elegant, peppery undertone. The C&Z cake will do well on its own in the afternoon, or for dessert, with a scoop of yogurt gelato.

1. Preheat the oven to 350°F and grease a 10-inch springform pan with butter or oil.

2. In a large mixing bowl, whisk together the flour, cocoa powder, baking soda, baking powder, and salt. In a food processor, process the sugar and butter until creamy (you can also do this by hand, armed with a sturdy spatula). Add the vanilla, coffee granules, and eggs, mixing well between each addition.

3. Reserve a cup of the flour mixture and add the rest to the egg mixture. Mix until just combined; the batter will be thick.

4. Add the zucchini and chocolate chips to the reserved flour mixture and toss to coat. Fold into the batter and blend with a wooden spoon — don't overmix. Pour into the prepared cake pan and level the surface with a spatula.

5. Bake for 40 to 50 minutes, until a knife inserted in the center comes out clean. Transfer to a rack to cool for 10 minutes, run a knife around the pan to loosen the cake, and unclasp the sides of the pan. Let cool to room temperature before serving. Sprinkle with confectioners' sugar, glaze with melted chocolate, or decorate with a few slices of raw zucchini (you don't have to eat them, though).

$1/2$ cup (1 stick) unsalted butter at room temperature, or $1/2$ cup extra virgin olive oil, plus 1 pat butter or teaspoon olive oil for greasing

2 cups all-purpose flour

$1/2$ cup unsweetened Dutch-process cocoa powder

1 teaspoon baking soda

$1/2$ teaspoon baking powder

$1/2$ teaspoon fine sea salt

1 cup (packed) light brown sugar

1 teaspoon pure vanilla extract

1 teaspoon instant coffee granules

3 large eggs

2 cups unpeeled grated zucchini, from about $1 1/2$ medium zucchini (keep the remaining $1/2$ zucchini for optional garnish)

1 cup good-quality bittersweet chocolate chips

Confectioners' sugar or melted bittersweet chocolate (optional)

Serves 12

WINE MAURY MAS AMIEL CUVÉE SPÉCIALE 10 ANS D'ÂGE (France, Languedoc-Roussillon, fortified red) This *vin doux naturel* has a portlike nose of prune and cocoa, a light, yet velvety texture, and warm flavors of ripe fruit and caramel.

Gâteau Chocolat & Courgette
Chocolate & Zucchini Cake, page 166

Gâteau Chocolat Framboise
Chocolate Raspberry Cake, page 170

Gâteau Ricotta, Abricot & Pistache
Apricot and Pistachio Ricotta Cake, page 171

GÂTEAU CHOCOLAT FRAMBOISE

Chocolate Raspberry Cake

*L*ike most die-hard chocolate fans, I swoon over rich, dense, and fudgy chocolate cakes, when the dark intensity of each bite washes over you with an audible swoosh.

While I would gladly sell my soul for a straight shot (no ice) of melt-in-your-mouth chocolate cake, I equally enjoy this variation, in which mashed raspberries are folded into the batter. The outcome is just as ferociously chocolaty, but the raspberries add a flowery tingle that reveals itself in the aftermath of the chocolate wave.

Make it a day ahead, to give the flavors time to ripen, and serve it with fresh raspberries; a dollop of crème fraîche or creamy yogurt is also welcome. It is sumptuously rich and a sliver is usually enough to satisfy serious chocolate cravings, but I've certainly been known to consume more than my fair share.

1/2 pound (2 sticks) unsalted butter, plus a
   pat to grease the pan

8 ounces good-quality bittersweet
   chocolate

1 cup sugar

4 large eggs

1 1/2 cups raspberries (thawed if frozen),
   plus a dozen for garnish, about 1 pint
   total

1/3 cup all-purpose flour

1 teaspoon fleur de sel or kosher salt (or
   1/2 teaspoon fine sea salt)

Serves 12
Chilling time: 8 hours

1. Preheat the oven to 350°F and grease a 10-inch springform pan with the pat of butter.

2. Melt the chocolate and the rest of the butter in a double boiler, or in a heatproof bowl set over a pan of simmering water, stirring from time to time to combine. Transfer the chocolate mixture into a medium mixing bowl, add the sugar, and stir with a wooden spoon. Let cool for 5 minutes. Add the eggs one by one, stirring well between each addition.

3. Mash the raspberries roughly with a fork. If the raspberries have large seeds, you can strain the raspberry mixture through a medium-mesh sieve into a

bowl and use only the pulp and juices, but this is optional. Add the raspberries to the batter. Sift in the flour, add the salt, and stir until combined.

4. Pour the batter into the prepared pan and bake for 30 minutes. Turn the oven off and leave the cake in the closed oven for another 5 minutes. Transfer the pan to a cooling rack, run a knife around the pan to loosen the cake, and unclasp the sides of the pan. Let cool completely, cover tightly with plastic wrap, and refrigerate for 8 hours or overnight. Remove from the refrigerator 30 minutes before serving and garnish with fresh raspberries.

VARIATIONS Replace the raspberries with diced mango, black currants (crushed and strained to remove the seeds), or black cherries (pitted and chopped), or omit the fruit altogether. If you like liquor in your chocolate, add a tablespoon to the batter — port with raspberries, light rum with mango, crème de cassis with black currants, and Armagnac with cherries. Or, instead of fruit, fold $^3/_4$ cup nuts into the batter, toasted and finely chopped.

WINE 2004 ROSA REGALE BRACHETTO D'ACQUI D.O.C.G. (Italy, Piedmont, sparkling red) This lightly sweet sparkler is low in alcohol, and its complex flavors are a rare match to dark chocolate. The fruity notes of raspberry, strawberry, and rose petals respond to the mashed raspberries, and the bubbles curb the richness of the cake.

GÂTEAU RICOTTA, ABRICOT & PISTACHE

Apricot and Pistachio Ricotta Cake

Le goûter (goo-tay) is French for an afternoon snack, the one that tides you over from lunch until dinner. Children are the most observant of this custom and can often be seen walking home from school nibbling on a *croissant* or a brioche, with an optional stick of chocolate thrust into it. Another name for *le goûter* is *le quatre-heures* (four o'clock), which refers to the time at which kids are traditionally let out of class.

At my parents' house, it is practically an institution, and the day is not quite complete unless we gather around the coffee table, cross-legged on the carpet or nestled in the couch, to eat something sweet and wash it down with gallons of tea. When I was a senior in high school — the year I suddenly discovered, with great displeasure, that some subjects actually required a bit of studying on my part — it was the promise of this soon-to-come *goûter* that kept me sane as I worked my weekends away, preparing for the graduation exams. That, and the bar of dark chocolate with caramelized hazelnuts in the top drawer of my desk, but don't tell anyone.

I was so fond of this late-afternoon break that I took the habit with me when I moved out. More often than not I have something virtuous and healthy (when the fairies gathered around my cradle, they blessed me with a sincere appreciation for apples), but on weekends and whenever I get a chance, I like to have friends or family over for *le goûter* and bake a little something for us.

This ricotta cake is terrific for such occasions: topped with toasted pistachios and sweet-tart apricots, it has a hearty and satisfying crumb that makes it the perfect partner for a cup of tea — especially rooibos, an earthy red tea from South Africa.

1/2 cup (1 stick) unsalted butter at room temperature, plus 1 pat to grease the pan

1 cup plus 1 tablespoon sugar

3 large eggs

1 cup whole-milk ricotta, preferably artisanal

1 teaspoon pure vanilla extract

2 1/2 cups all-purpose flour

1/2 teaspoon fine sea salt

2 teaspoons baking powder

1 tablespoon (loosely packed) finely grated orange zest, from an organic orange

2/3 cup shelled unsalted pistachios, toasted and chopped (available from gourmet or natural foods stores, or Middle Eastern markets; if you can only find salted pistachios, see page 80)

12 fresh and ripe apricots, halved (substitute frozen apricot halves, no thawing necessary)

Serves 8 to 10

1. Preheat the oven to 350°F and grease a 10-inch springform pan with the pat of butter.

2. In a food processor (or in a large mixing bowl if you choose to do this by hand), combine the remaining butter and the 1 cup sugar and process until creamy. Add the eggs one by one, the ricotta, and the vanilla extract and mix between each addition.

3. In a medium mixing bowl, sift together the flour, salt, and baking powder. Add the flour mixture and orange zest to the egg mixture. Mix until just combined;

the batter will be thick. Fold in half of the pistachios (reserve the other half for top-ping) and pour the batter into the prepared pan, leveling the surface with a spatula.

4. Arrange the apricots skin side down over the batter in a regular pattern. It's okay to crowd them a little; they will shrink as they bake. Sprinkle with the remaining table-spoon of sugar and the remaining pistachios.

5. Bake for 1 hour, until a knife inserted in the center comes out clean. Transfer the pan to a cooling rack and let rest for 10 minutes. Run a knife around the pan to loosen the cake, unclasp the sides of the pan, and let cool completely before serving. The cake tastes best fresh out of the oven, but it will keep for 2 days at room temper-ature, wrapped tightly in foil.

VARIATIONS Instead of apricots and pistachios, try pears and walnuts, apples and hazel-nuts, or fresh figs and almonds.

LE GÂTEAU DE MAMY

My Grandmother's Apple Cake

$\mathcal{T}$his is a recipe that my paternal grandmother gave to my mother, and we just call it *le gâteau de Mamy* (my sister insists that it is Mamie, not Mamy, but this is my book and I will spell it as I please). She herself had gotten it decades ago from her dear and much missed friend Ella so she refers to it as *le gâteau d'Ella*, and the chain of names probably goes on to the beginning of time. Whatever one chooses to call it, it is a de-light for tea or dessert in the fall and winter; a golden, buttery apple cake with soft fruit chunks that melt on your tongue, and crisp edges that you should save for last.

1. Preheat the oven to 350°F. Melt the butter in a small saucepan or in a nonmetal-lic bowl set in the microwave. Grease a nonstick 8-inch round cake pan (not spring-form) with 1 tablespoon of the butter using a pastry brush or paper towel.

$^1/_2$ cup (1 stick) plus 1 tablespoon unsalted butter

$^1/_2$ cup all-purpose flour

1 teaspoon baking powder

$^1/_4$ teaspoon fine sea salt

1 pound baking apples, such as Braeburn, Jonagold, or Pippin, about 2 medium

$^3/_4$ cup sugar

2 large eggs

Serves 6 to 8

2. Combine the flour, baking powder, and salt in a small mixing bowl. Wash, peel, and core the apples. Cut them in eighths and arrange over the bottom of the pan.

3. In a medium mixing bowl, whisk the sugar with the eggs until fluffy. Add the flour mixture and whisk until combined. Add the melted butter and whisk again until blended. Pour the batter evenly over the fruit and bake for 40 minutes, until the top is set and golden brown.

4. Let the cake settle on a cooling rack for 10 minutes. Run a knife around the pan to loosen and flip the cake onto a plate; if any piece of fruit has stuck to the bottom of the pan, scrape it off carefully and place it back on the cake where it belongs. Flip the cake again onto a serving plate — work cautiously so as not to squish the cake between the two plates. Let cool and serve slightly warm or at room temperature.

VARIATIONS This cake can also be made with pears, quince, apricots, or nectarines. For a slight change of texture and flavor, reduce the amount of butter by 2 tablespoons, and grind the sugar with $^1/_4$ cup whole blanched almonds before you mix it with the eggs.

PAIN D'ÉPICE

Honey Spice Loaf

There is a tiny shop in Paris, perched on top of the bucolic Butte-aux-Cailles hill, which specializes in honey products and beekeeping gear. I had walked past it countless times as it was very close to my office, but it never seemed to be open. Occasionally a handwritten sign would be duct-taped to the door, proclaiming, "I am at the café next door if you need me." Not wanting to violate the sanctity of a coffee break, I would just walk away with a little sigh.

But on a balmy September day there was light inside, and since I was in no hurry to return to work after my lunch date, I pushed the door open and stepped inside. The walls were lined from floor to ceiling with jars of honey — dozens of different kinds, in sundry shades of gold and amber — and all the equipment you would need to raise your own bee colony if such was your fancy and you weren't allergic to bee stings. And there, on a table, was a very large and very tempting slab of *pain d'épice*, with a big knife and a few scattered crumbs next to it.

Pain d'épice is a traditional French cake flavored with honey and spices, usually baked in a loaf pan. It can be purchased at any French grocery store, pre-sliced and wrapped in plastic, a little dull and a little dry, and until then I believed that this was all you could expect from it. But this looked quite different.

The owner of the shop, a gruff old man with exactly the kind of bearlike beard you would imagine on a beekeeper, followed my gaze and, to my surprise, offered me a sliver to taste. I gladly accepted, smelled it, took a bite, and this first taste of true, artisanal pain d'épice came as a shock, an epiphany. Such warmth of flavor, such aromas, it was a whole jar of honey and your entire spice rack captured in one moist cake — how had I lived without it for so long?

From that point on, I could never go back to ordinary pain d'épice. But I do return to that store whenever I'm in the neighborhood, I taste every pain d'épice that crosses my path when I travel (any French region that produces honey is likely to offer a good loaf), and I also bake my own version, after many a trial to find just the taste and texture I was looking for. I like to add candied orange peel or ginger for extra jolts of flavor, but both are something of an acquired taste, so you can omit them if you like.

Pain d'épice is quite felicitous for breakfast, particularly on bleak winter mornings when you could use a pick-me-up. Some people spread it with salted butter, but I just toast a slice or two and eat them with a juicy pear. Pain d'épice is just as fine as an afternoon snack, it can be cut in cubes and served with coffee at the end of a meal, and its warm spiciness makes it fit for the holiday season. It also finds its place in savory recipes — in thin slivers with foie gras, in a stuffing for poultry, or in the Flemish Carbonades recipe on page 134 (see variation).

2 teaspoons vegetable oil to grease the pan

1 1/2 cups milk

2/3 cup good-quality honey (grease the measuring cup with a bit of vegetable oil before measuring; the honey will slip right out)

1/3 cup mild-flavored dark molasses (use the same measuring cup trick)

1 cup all-purpose flour

1 cup whole wheat flour

2 teaspoons baking powder

1 teaspoon baking soda

1/4 teaspoon fine sea salt

2 teaspoons French four-spice mix (or 1/2 teaspoon each of ground cinnamon, ground cloves, ground nutmeg, and ground ginger)

Optional: 1/4 cup finely diced candied ginger (look for the tender and moist kind, which can be found in Asian stores), or 1/4 cup finely diced candied orange peel, or a mix of the two

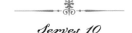

Serves 10
Resting time: 12 hours

You should bake the loaf a day ahead, to give the honey and spices time to bloom. The taste varies depending on how the slices are cut, thick or thin, so try both and see what you prefer.

1. Preheat the oven to 350°F. Grease the bottom and sides of a 9 by 5-inch loaf pan with oil, and line the bottom with parchment paper.

2. Combine the milk, honey, and molasses in a small saucepan. Set over medium heat and heat the mixture without boiling, stirring with a spatula until dissolved. Set aside and let cool as you go on with the recipe.

3. In a large mixing bowl, combine the flours, baking powder, baking soda, salt, and spices. In a small bowl, combine the ginger and/or orange peel, if using, with 2 teaspoons of the flour mixture and set aside.

4. Form a well in the center of the flour mixture. Pour in the milk mixture slowly and whisk in a circular motion, starting from the center, until all the flour has been incorporated — the batter will be thin. Fold in the ginger and/or orange peel, if using. Pour the batter

Pain d'Épice
Honey Spice Loaf

into the prepared loaf pan and bake for 40 to 50 minutes, until the surface is brown and a knife inserted in the center comes out clean.

5. Transfer to a rack to cool for 20 minutes. Run a knife along the sides of the pan to loosen the loaf, and unmold. Let cool completely, wrap in foil, and let rest at room temperature until the next day.

GÂTEAU AU YAOURT

Yogurt Cake

Gâteau au yaourt is a staple of French home baking. Very easy to make and even easier to love, it is a moist and cloudlike cake, not too sweet, and just perfect for any time of day. Breakfast, tea, dessert — any time at all, trust me. The recipe calls for two French-sized tubs of yogurt (equivalent to a cup) that you use, once empty, to measure the rest of the ingredients. This no-scale approach is a notable exception to the modern French usage, in which quantities are measured by weight rather than volume.

Yogurt cake is very popular with kids, who love a simple, clean-flavored cake, but what they enjoy the most is that they can mix the batter entirely on their own — I do suggest a bit of supervision, so no harm will befall your kitchen or your child. In fact, yogurt cake is often the first cake that French children learn to make: I baked my first in kindergarten, where we had a teacher named Madame Marguerite (whom I didn't like despite her novel-worthy name) and a cool kitchen, scaled down to our size. My mother still has the recipe I wrote then in untidy caps, but I must have copied it a bit distractedly because it calls for a lot of oil and no sugar. Fortunately, Maxence's grandmother has given me hers, and it is the one I use now.

The basic yogurt cake recipe can be tinkered with endlessly. You can add citrus juice or zest to the batter; fold in berries, chocolate chips, or nuts; substitute ground almonds or cocoa powder for part of the flour; slice the cake in two and spread raspberry jam, lemon curd, or ganache in the middle; or dress the cake with whatever frosting or glaze you like. But gâteau au yaourt is Maxence's all-time favorite cake — which is why I secured his grandmother's recipe in the first place — and he is a big advocate of the adage "If it ain't broke, don't fix it." I seem to have trouble following these words of wisdom — substitution is my middle name — but every time I go back to the original, unadulterated gâteau au yaourt, I am reminded that its delightful simplicity is well worth the suppression of my creative impulses.

Yogurt cake can be eaten fresh out of the oven or at room temperature. If you serve the basic version for dessert, you can accessorize it with the Raspberry Coulis on page 204. The cake will keep well for a few days at room temperature, wrapped in foil: the flavors will develop and the top will soften, turning silky on the tongue.

1. Preheat the oven to 350°F. Grease the sides of a 10-inch round cake pan or springform pan with oil and line the bottom with parchment paper if the pan is not springform.

2. In a large mixing bowl, whisk together the yogurt and sugar. Add the eggs one by one, beating well after each addition. Add the vanilla, oil, and rum, if using, and whisk again.

3. In another bowl, sift together the flour, baking powder, baking soda, and salt. Pour the flour mixture into the yogurt mixture, and whisk until just combined.

4. Pour the batter into the prepared cake pan and bake for 35 to 40 minutes, until the top is golden brown and a knife inserted in the center comes out clean. Transfer the pan to a cooling rack and let stand for 10 minutes. Run a knife around the pan to loosen. If you're using a springform pan, unclasp the sides. Otherwise, flip the cake onto a plate and flip it back on the rack. Serve slightly warm or at room temperature.

$1/3$ cup vegetable oil, plus 1 teaspoon to grease the pan

1 cup plain unsweetened yogurt, preferably whole milk

1 cup sugar

2 large eggs

1 teaspoon pure vanilla extract

1 tablespoon light or amber rum (optional but recommended)

$1^2/3$ cups all-purpose flour

$1^1/2$ teaspoons baking powder

1 teaspoon baking soda

A good pinch of fine sea salt

❋

Serves 8 to 10

Tartes

TARTS

Pâte Sablée

SHORT PASTRY

Tarte Nectarine & Pêche au Gingembre

NECTARINE, PEACH, AND GINGER TART

Tartelettes aux Fraises

STRAWBERRY TARTLETS

Tarte Amandine à la Myrtille

BLUEBERRY AMANDINE TART

Tarte Tatin

APPLE TATIN

Tarte Chocolat Caramel

CHOCOLATE CARAMEL TART

PÂTE SABLÉE

Short Pastry

𝒯here are many things for which I am grateful to my mother. The gift of life ranks quite high — a precious thing, that — but her basic tart crust recipe is a close second. This recipe does not involve the usual daunting steps of rolling out a stubborn dough and transferring it awkwardly into the pan: instead, my mother's method has you combining all the ingredients into a sandy mixture that you simply dump in the pan and pack with your fingers to form a crust, like you would for a cheesecake.

Since it is hand shaped, the result is not as prom-queen perfect as what you'd expect from a pastry shop: the rims may be a bit ruffled and uneven, but it is this very imperfection that makes it so expressive and so appetizing. That, and the fact that it bakes into a golden shell, so crisp and sandy you might be tempted to eat it on its own.

$1/3$ cup sugar

1 cup plus 2 tablespoons all-purpose flour

$1/4$ teaspoon fine sea salt

7 tablespoons ($3^1/2$ ounces) chilled unsalted butter, diced, plus a pat to grease the pan

1 to 2 tablespoons cold milk

*Makes enough to line a
10-inch tart pan, or six
4-inch tartlet molds
Chilling time: 30 minutes*

1. Grease a 10-inch tart or quiche pan with butter.

2. **If working with a food processor,** combine the sugar, flour, and salt in the processor. Add the butter and process in short pulses, until the mixture resembles coarse meal. Add a tablespoon of milk and process again, in short pulses, until the milk is absorbed. The dough should still be crumbly, but it should clump if you gently squeeze a handful in your hand. If it doesn't, add a little more milk, teaspoon by teaspoon, and give the dough a few more pulses, until it reaches the desired consistency. Proceed to step 3.

If working by hand, in a medium mixing bowl, combine the sugar, flour, and salt. Add the butter and rub it into the dry ingredients with the tips of your fingers or a wire pastry blender, until the mixture resembles coarse meal. Add a tablespoon of milk and blend it in, handling the dough as lightly as you can. The dough should still be crumbly, but it should clump if you gently squeeze a handful in your hand. If it doesn't, add a little more milk, teaspoon by teaspoon, and blend again, still working lightly, until it reaches the desired consistency. Proceed to step 3.

3. Pour the mixture into the prepared tart pan and use the back of a tablespoon to spread it evenly over the bottom. Using the heels of your hands and your fingers, press down on the dough to form a thin layer, covering the surface of the pan and creating a rim all around. Don't worry if the dough feels a little dry—this is normal. Cover with plastic wrap and refrigerate for 30 minutes, or up to a day.

VARIATIONS Flavor the dough with 1 teaspoon vanilla extract or finely grated citrus zest, $^1/2$ teaspoon spice (nutmeg, cinnamon, ginger), or 1 teaspoon liqueur (Grand Marnier, Cointreau, rum). Add these ingredients along with the butter.

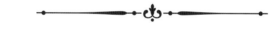

TARTE NECTARINE & PÊCHE AU GINGEMBRE

Nectarine, Peach, and Ginger Tart

Smooth skinned, warmly sweet, and the color of sunshine, yellow nectarines have been my most cherished summer fruit for as long as I can remember. I am quite content to eat them by the crate and out of hand, licking the juices that run down my wrist before they reach my sleeve, but they lend themselves remarkably well to baking, too. A short vacation in the oven turns their slippery flesh to velvet and gives their flavor a lightly caramelized aura. In this tart, yellow nectarines are paired with white peaches and ginger, a talented trio that balances the sweet, the tangy, and the subtly fiery.

1. Peel the ginger and grate it using the small holes of a cheese grater. Discard the woody fibers and save the pulp and juice. Prepare the Pâte Sablée according to the instructions on page 182, adding the ginger's pulp and juice at the same time as the

FOR THE PÂTE SABLÉE

A knob of fresh ginger, about 1 inch in length

1/3 cup sugar

1 cup plus 2 tablespoons all-purpose flour

1/4 teaspoon fine sea salt

7 tablespoons (3 1/2 ounces) chilled unsalted butter, diced, plus a pat to grease the pan

1 to 2 tablespoons cold milk

FOR THE FILLING

2 ripe white peaches, about 7 ounces each

3 ripe yellow nectarines, about 7 ounces each

2 tablespoons good-quality candied ginger (look for the soft and moist kind, which can be found at Asian markets)

2 tablespoons sour cream or crème fraîche

1 large egg

1 to 3 tablespoons light brown sugar, depending on how sweet your fruit is

Serves 10
Chilling time: 30 minutes
for the dough

butter. Line a 10-inch tart pan with the dough as instructed, cover with plastic wrap, and refrigerate for 30 minutes, or up to a day.

2. Preheat the oven to 350°F. Bake the tart shell for 15 to 20 minutes, until golden, keeping an eye on it.

3. While the dough bakes, peel the peaches (this is easier if you blanch them first by putting them in a pan of simmering water for a minute); no need to peel the nectarines. Core and slice the fruit, about 12 slices per fruit, and put the slices in a colander to drain for 15 minutes if they are very juicy. (Save the juices to drink.)

4. Dice the candied ginger finely and set aside. In a medium mixing bowl, whisk together the cream and egg.

5. When the crust is golden, remove it from the oven (leave the heat on) and let cool for 5 minutes. Arrange the fruit in a circular pattern over the crust, starting from the outside. Pour the egg mixture evenly over the fruit; it will look a little thin. Sprinkle with brown sugar — 1 tablespoon if the fruit is very sweet, 2 or 3 if it isn't — and candied ginger.

6. Bake for 25 minutes, until the fruit is softened. Turn off the oven and leave the tart in the closed oven for another 10 minutes. Transfer to a rack to cool completely before serving. (The tart can be prepared up to 8 hours ahead. Cover with foil and keep at room temperature.)

*W*INE MARCO NEGRI 2004 MOSCATO D'ASTI (Italy, Piedmont, sparkling white) Low in alcohol and only slightly fizzy, this wine offers fruity flavors of peach and citrus, fragrant floral notes, and a fresh acidity. It is soft and creamy in the mouth.

TARTELETTES AUX FRAISES

Strawberry Tartlets

$\mathscr{C}$onsidering that my mother holds the secret to the world's best crust recipe (Biased? *Moi?*), it is really no surprise that she should be such a terrific tart baker: blueberries and apricots in the summer, blackberries and plums in the fall, pears and apples in the winter, and I don't care what the calendar says, it's not really spring until she makes a strawberry tart.

When the first of the berries appear in the market and I get the urge to bake one myself, I like to prepare little tartlets (they're fun to assemble and so pleasing to the eye), but the result provides essentially the same sweet satisfaction: a thin crisp crust and a fresh layer of pastry cream form the perfect jewelry box for the glistening ruby of strawberries. (If you don't have tartlet molds, you can either run out and buy a set or use the same recipe to make a 10-inch tart.)

1. Prepare the Pâte Sablée and line six 4-inch tartlet molds as instructed. Make sure the dough is spread thinly; depending on the shape and depth of your molds, you may not have to use all of it. Cover with plastic wrap and refrigerate for 30 minutes, or up to a day. (Any leftover dough can be sprinkled over fruit chunks in a ramekin and baked as for a crumble.)

2. Preheat the oven to 350°F. Bake the tartlet shells for 12 to 14 minutes, until golden, keeping an eye on them. Remove from the oven and let cool.

3. **Prepare the pastry cream (crème pâtissière):** in a medium mixing bowl, whisk together the egg, vanilla, and sugar. Whisk in the cornstarch and set aside. In a

Pâte Sablée (page 182)

1 large egg

1 teaspoon pure vanilla extract

2 tablespoons sugar

2 tablespoons cornstarch

$^1/_2$ cup milk

4 cups fresh strawberries, about 2 pints

Serves 6
Resting/chilling time:
30 minutes for the dough,
1 hour for the pastry
cream

Tarte Nectarine & Pêche au Gingembre
Nectarine, Peach, and Ginger Tart, page 183

Tarte Amandine à la Myrtille
Blueberry Amandine Tart, page 188

medium saucepan, bring the milk to a simmer over medium heat. As soon as the milk simmers, pour it into the egg mixture, whisk vigorously until blended, and pour the mixture back into the saucepan. Return the saucepan to low heat, and whisk for 30 seconds as it thickens. Spoon the crème pâtissière into the prepared tartlet shells, level the surface with a spoon, and let cool completely on the counter, about an hour.

4. Rinse the strawberries, pat them dry, and hull them. Cut the strawberries lengthwise in halves or quarters, depending on their size. Arrange the fruit on the crème pâtissière in a circular pattern, starting from the center. Serve immediately, or cover with plastic wrap and refrigerate for up to 8 hours. Bring to room temperature before serving.

VARIATIONS These tartlets can be made with other varieties of fresh fruit: raspberries in the summer, figs in the fall, and kiwi or pineapple in the winter.

WINE CODORNIU PINOT NOIR ROSÉ NV (Spain, Catalonia, sparkling rosé) This dry rosé bubbly is bright, refreshing, and flavorful. Pretty and pink, it offers flavors of strawberry with notes of raspberry and a delightful citrus finish.

TARTE AMANDINE À LA MYRTILLE

Blueberry Amandine Tart

When I was little, my family would spend three weeks in the French Alps every summer, renting a cabin in a different village each year. At the time, I wished we would just drive to the beach like everyone else instead of hiking up and down steep trails and swimming in ice-cold lakes, but my parents preferred the quiet of heights to the clammy crowds of beach resorts, and I think I see their point now.

Many rituals surrounded these summer getaways: the purchase of new hiking shoes when our feet had outgrown the old ones, games of Crazy Eights to while away the mountain downpours, and pastries from the local bakery in late afternoon. I was a creature of habit at the time, and my pastry of choice, the one I would pick day in, day out, was the amandine: an almond cream tartlet topped with sliced almonds and half a candied cherry. The cherry I usually discarded, or generously donated to my mother, but the tartlet I devoured, ravenous from the day's hike, biting in and admiring the neat imprint of my teeth.

The following tart is a variation on the amandine from my childhood. A layer of blueberries lies beneath the smooth almond filling, melding into it and creating a handsome contrast in the cut slices. It is the sort of tart that your guests will assume you bought from a pastry shop, so find a way to mention casually, in the course of the conversation, that you did bake it from scratch.

1. Prepare the Pâte Sablée and line a 10-inch tart pan as instructed. Cover with plastic wrap and refrigerate for at least 30 minutes, or up to a day.

2. Preheat the oven to 350°F. Bake the tart shell for 10 to 12 minutes, until lightly golden. Remove the pan from the oven (leave the heat on) and transfer to a rack to cool for 10 minutes.

3. **Prepare the almond cream (crème d'amande):** combine the sugar, almonds, and salt in a food processor and mix until finely ground. Add the butter and process until combined. Add the eggs one by one and mix until smooth. This can be made up to a day ahead: transfer to an airtight container and refrigerate. Bring to room temperature before using.

Pâte Sablée (page 182)

$^1/_2$ cup sugar

$^3/_4$ cup whole blanched almonds

$^1/_4$ teaspoon fine sea salt

8 tablespoons (1 stick) unsalted butter, at room temperature

2 large eggs

2 cups blueberries, fresh or frozen (no need to thaw them if they are frozen)

$^1/_3$ cup sliced almonds

❈

Serves 10
Chilling time: 30 minutes
for the dough

4. Pour the blueberries in the tart shell, cover evenly with crème d'amande, and level the surface with a spatula, working gently to avoid popping the blueberries.

5. Back for 25 minutes. Take the pan out, sprinkle with sliced almonds, and bake for 15 minutes, until the crème d'amande is set and the almonds are golden. Let cool completely and serve. (The tart can be made up to 8 hours ahead, covered with foil, and refrigerated. Bring to room temperature before serving.)

VARIATIONS Replace the blueberries with slivers of poached pear or mashed raspberries, or omit the fruit altogether.

*W*INE GRAHAM SIX GRAPES PORT (Portugal, Porto, fortified red) This great-value port shows excellent balance: it is sweet and rather fruity, with red berry flavors and nutty, toasted notes. An aged vintage port will be pricier but smoother.

TARTE TATIN

A classic of French pastry if there ever was one, *tarte tatin* is often featured on the menu at Parisian restaurants. But however much I love a warm upside-down apple tart, I rarely order it when I eat out. Why is that, you ask? Because most restaurants insist on using puff pastry (*pâte feuilletée*) instead of a nice, honest-to-goodness short pastry.

Don't get me wrong, puff pastry is a must in certain confections (*mille-feuille* and *galette des rois* spring to mind), but among my idiosyncratic food beliefs is this one: a tarte tatin needs a crust with broad enough shoulders to stand up to the fruit. Not a thin and flimsy one that will get soaked and bullied into oblivion.

So before I order, I always ask what type of pastry they use for their tarte tatin. This invariably irks the waiter, who has to go into the kitchen and ask. Ninety-nine percent of the time he comes back to tell me that it is puff pastry, and I end up choosing something else, saving myself for this homemade version: soft apples, buttery salted caramel, and a generous crust, slowly imbued with (not obliterated by) the juices seeping from the fruit.

Some people like their tatin with crème fraîche or vanilla ice cream, but I think a good tatin needs no embellishment and I prefer it on its own. My mother's Pâte Sablée (page 182) cannot be used for this tart since the dough needs to be rolled out and laid over the fruit, but don't let that deter you: proceed carefully and without fear, work on a well-floured surface, and you will be just fine.

1. **Prepare the dough:** in a medium mixing bowl, combine the sugar, flour, and salt. Add the butter and rub it into the dry ingredients with the tips of your fingers or a wire pastry blender, until the mixture resembles coarse meal. Add 1 tablespoon milk, and knead the dough gently until it forms a smooth ball. If the dough does not come together after a minute, add a dash more milk, teaspoon by teaspoon, and knead again. (Alternatively, this can be done in a food processor.) Gather into a ball, flatten slightly, wrap in plastic, and refrigerate for 30 minutes.

2. Butter the sides of a 9- or 10-inch cake pan (not springform) or quiche pan with the pat of butter.

3. Combine the brown sugar and 1 tablespoon water in a small heavy-bottomed saucepan and melt the sugar slowly over medium-low heat. Swish the pan around from time to time, but don't stir. As soon as bubbles form on the surface (avoid overcooking the caramel, which would result in a bitter aftertaste), remove from heat. Add the salt and butter and stir with a wooden spoon until the butter is melted and blended into a paste with the caramel. Pour immediately into the pan and use the back of your spoon to spread it over the bottom of the pan. The entire surface need not be covered, but make it as even as you can. Set aside.

4. Preheat the oven to 350°F and remove the dough from the fridge. Rinse, core, peel, and slice the apples in eighths. Arrange the apple pieces in a circular pattern over the caramel in the pan, starting from the outside.

5. Roll out the dough into a circle, about 10 inches in diameter if you use a 9-inch pan, 11 inches if you use a 10-inch pan. Prick the dough all over with a fork. Fold it loosely over the rolling pin, lay it over the apples in the pan, and tuck in the overhanging flaps of dough.

FOR THE DOUGH

$^1/_2$ cup sugar

1$^1/_4$ cups all-purpose flour, sifted

$^1/_4$ teaspoon fine sea salt

8 tablespoons (1 stick) chilled unsalted butter, diced, plus a pat for greasing the pan

1 to 2 tablespoons milk

FOR THE CARAMEL AND FILLING

$^1/_3$ cup (packed) light brown sugar

$^1/_4$ teaspoon fine sea salt

3 tablespoons unsalted butter, at room temperature

2 pounds baking apples, such as Braeburn, Jonagold, or Pippin, about 4 medium

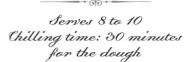

*Serves 8 to 10
Chilling time: 30 minutes
for the dough*

6. Bake the tart for 45 minutes to an hour, until the dough turns golden and your house is filled with the smell of caramelized apples.

7. Take the pan out of the oven, run a knife around the sides to loosen the crust, and flip onto a serving dish. If some apple pieces stick to the bottom of the pan, just scrape them off and place them back on the tart where they belong. Serve warm, but not piping hot. (The tart can be made up to 8 hours ahead. Cover with foil and keep at room temperature. Reheat for 15 minutes in a 350°F oven before serving.)

*W*INE PETIT-VÉDRINES SAUTERNES 2002 (France, Bordeaux, fortified white) This Sauternes is rich with flavors of honey, burnt sugar, and caramel. It is sweet, but not overly so, with a well-rounded acidity. It is also worth splurging on a bottle of ice cider from Quebec, such as Neige by La Face Cachée de la Pomme: full-bodied and silky on the palate, it offers clean flavors of fresh apple, honey, and candied fruit.

TARTE CHOCOLAT CARAMEL

Chocolate Caramel Tart

*A*nyone who's serious about pastry shops needs a reliable benchmark by which to judge, grade, and classify them. For some it might be the coffee *éclair* (the dough should be crisp but giving, the filling should have an assertive coffee flavor and not taste eggy, and the glaze should be sweet and thick but neither cloying nor sticky on the roof of your mouth) or perhaps the *mille-feuille* (the puff pastry should dissolve into light flakes and not feel dry or brittle, the vanilla cream should have the distinctive flavor of real beans, and the ratio of cream to pastry should be roughly two thirds, so you will make a mess eating it — that can't be helped — but won't have all the cream squish out onto your lap).

For me, the ultimate benchmark is the chocolate tart. Be it a single-serving tartlet or a slice of a larger tart, I am attentive to the quality of the ganache, which should be intensely flavored but not too thick, too soft, or too gelled, and the delicate crust, which should be sandy, and just sweet enough to tease the bitterness of the chocolate.

But for all the chocolate tarts and tartlets that I taste here and there I can never get enough, and this handsome dessert remains one of my favorites to make at home. I have experimented with many a variation, but this one, hiding a layer of salted caramel beneath the chocolate blanket, is undisputedly the most acclaimed. As you might imagine it is an indulgent affair, and a small slice is enough to fill you with a sense of deep, lip-smacking satisfaction.

1. Grease a 10-inch tart pan with butter. Prepare the Pâte Sablée and line the pan as instructed. Wrap tightly with plastic and refrigerate for 30 minutes, or up to a day.

2. Preheat the oven to 350°F. Bake for 20 to 25 minutes, until golden, keeping an eye on it. Transfer to a rack to cool.

3. **Prepare the caramel filling:** make sure you have all the ingredients measured out before you start. Combine the brown sugar and 1 tablespoon water in a small heavy-bottomed saucepan and melt the sugar slowly over medium-low heat. Swish the pan around from time to time to ensure even melting, but don't stir. As soon as bubbles form on the surface (avoid overcooking the caramel, which would result in a bitter taste afterward), add the honey and stir to combine. Add the salt and cream and stir until blended. Remove from heat, add the butter, and stir to combine. Pour the caramel into the tart shell and tilt the pan slowly in a circular motion to coat the bottom of the shell evenly. Let set in the fridge for 40 minutes.

4. **Prepare the ganache filling:** put the chocolate in a medium mixing bowl, preferably stainless steel. Bring

Pâte Sablée (page 182)

FOR THE CARAMEL FILLING

$^{1}/_{2}$ cup (packed) light brown sugar

1 tablespoon good-quality honey

$^{1}/_{2}$ teaspoon fleur de sel or kosher salt

$^{1}/_{3}$ cup crème fraîche or heavy cream

2 tablespoons unsalted butter, diced, plus a pat for greasing the pan

FOR THE GANACHE FILLING

10 ounces good-quality bittersweet chocolate, very finely chopped

1 cup crème fraîche or heavy cream

Serves 12 to 16
Chilling time: 30 minutes
for the dough, 40 minutes
for the caramel, 1 hour for
the finished tart

the cream to a simmer in a heavy-bottomed saucepan over medium-low heat. Pour half of the cream on the chocolate (cover the saucepan to keep the remaining cream warm), let stand for 20 seconds, and stir gently in the center with a whisk, gradually blending the cream with the chocolate until smooth. Add half of the remaining cream, and stir again until combined. Repeat with the remaining cream. Remove the tart pan from the fridge, pour the chocolate filling into the shell, and level the surface with a spatula. Return to the fridge to set for an hour.

5. Remove the tart from the fridge 15 minutes before serving. Cut in small slices — it is quite rich — and serve on its own, or with fresh berries. The leftovers will keep for 2 days, tightly wrapped and refrigerated.

VARIATIONS For the classic chocolate tart, omit the caramel layer. Or, instead of caramel, line the tart shell with fruit or preserves before you pour in the ganache, or sprinkle it with cacao nibs, toasted nuts, or crushed pralines. You can add liqueur, coffee, or spices (cardamom or ground ginger) to the ganache, or infuse the cream with tea (Earl Grey and Genmaicha in particular), citrus zest, or herbs (rosemary, bergamot, basil, lavender) before you use it for the ganache.

WINE BROADBENT NV RAINWATER MADEIRA (Portugal, Madeira, fortified white) This sweet dessert wine has a slight citrusy tartness, a great layering of flavors (fig, candied orange peel, burnt sugar, and butterscotch-caramel), and a deliciously nutty finish.

Tarte Chocolat Caramel
Chocolate Caramel Tart

Desserts

Crème Brûlée Chocolat Hibiscus
CHOCOLATE HIBISCUS CRÈME BRULÉE

*Blanc-Manger au Coulis de Basilic
ou Framboise*
BLANCMANGE WITH BASIL OR RASPBERRY COULIS

Brioche aux Amandes, Poire & Chocolat
ALMOND, PEAR, AND CHOCOLATE BRIOCHE

Compote d'Abricots à la Lavande
LAVENDER APRICOT COMPOTE

*Crème de Ricotta à la Mangue,
Croustillant de Macadamia*
CREAMY MANGO RICOTTA WITH
MACADAMIA CRUNCH

Crêpes

CRÈME BRÛLÉE CHOCOLAT HIBISCUS

Chocolate Hibiscus Crème Brûlée

*F*ew endeavors offer such gratification as re-creating a restaurant classic in your own kitchen, and crèmes brûlées definitely fall into that category: their creamy filling and fragile caramel crust, satisfyingly shattered by a light tap of the spoon, can be yours in just a few, none-too-difficult steps.

This is also good news for the gadget-oriented cook, who now has the perfect excuse to splurge on that chef's torch he's been coveting for so long at the fancy-schmancy cooking store. For a thriftier buy, you can also turn to the nearest hardware store and get a small, ordinary blowtorch — I bought mine from a tiny old *droguerie* in my neighborhood where the vacuum cleaner was obviously retired years ago. Whatever option you choose, as soon as you whip out your torch and melt some sugar with brio, your friends will start showing you the respect you deserve.

The basic crème brûlée is simply vanilla flavored and quite delicious as it is, but I find it much more attractive when it slips on a strapless chocolate gown. The following recipe has you steep dried hibiscus flowers in the custard. Their tart berry taste engages the chocolate in lively conversation and makes its fruitiness sparkle.

DRIED HIBISCUS FLOWERS

(sometimes marketed as flor de Jamaica*) are not really flowers, but rather the calyces of a plant called roselle, or red sorrel, from the hibiscus family. They can be steeped like tea leaves: the resulting beverage, vividly fuchsia, is a popular post-dinner tisane at my house, and a fine chilled drink to sip on during a heat wave. Dried hibiscus can be found in bulk or in teabags at organic and natural foods stores, Latin markets, or online. If you can't find it, substitute a good blend of black tea with berries or flowers, or omit it altogether.* ❧

1. Preheat the oven to 325°F.

2. Combine the cream and milk in a small saucepan. Bring to a simmer and remove from heat. Add the hibiscus and stir. Cover and let stand for 10 minutes.

3. Melt the chocolate in a double boiler, or in a heat-proof bowl set over a pan of simmering water, stirring from time to time to dissolve. Let cool slightly.

4. In a medium mixing bowl, whisk together the sugar and egg yolks. Add the chocolate and blend well. Pour the cream into the bowl through a fine-mesh sieve and discard the hibiscus. Blend well.

5. Pour into four 6-ounce ramekins, preferably wide and shallow, and place in a baking dish large enough to accommodate them. Pour very hot water into the dish to reach half the height of the ramekins (this prevents the custard from boiling).

6. Bake for 45 minutes, until the custard is set but still slightly wobbly in the center. Let rest in the baking dish

on the counter for 15 minutes before removing the ramekins (caution: they will still be hot). Let cool to room temperature, cover with plastic wrap, and chill for 2 hours, or up to a day. Remove from the fridge 30 minutes before serving.

7. Just before serving, sprinkle turbinado sugar over the surface of the custard. Place the ramekins on a nonflammable surface (your cooking range, for instance) and away from anything flammable. Use a blowtorch to melt and caramelize the sugar: be very cautious, follow the manufacturer's instructions if any, and keep the nozzle away from you or anyone you care about. Move the torch slowly over the sugar at a height of about 3 inches, moving it constantly to ensure an even caramelization. (Alternatively, you can put the ramekins in the oven under a very hot broiler for 2 minutes: the sugar won't melt as thoroughly, but it will form a slight crust nonetheless.) Let cool for a minute and serve.

*W*INE LES CLOS DE PAULILLES BANYULS RIMAGE 2003 (France, Languedoc-Roussillon, fortified red) Intensely red in the glass, this rich wine displays berry-dominated aromas that bring out the hibiscus notes in the custard. The flavors are similar, with hints of sweet spices and a chocolaty finish.

1¹/₂ cups light cream

¹/₂ cup milk

¹/₃ cup dried hibiscus flowers in bulk or 6 teabags of hibiscus (see page 198)

3 ounces good-quality bittersweet chocolate

¹/₃ cup sugar

3 large egg yolks

FOR THE CARAMEL CRUST

2 tablespoons turbinado sugar (coarse crystals of blond raw sugar) or light brown sugar

Serves 4
Chilling time: 2 hours

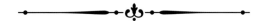

BLANC-MANGER AU COULIS DE BASILIC OU FRAMBOISE

Blancmange with Basil or Raspberry Coulis

*O*ld cookbooks are a fascinating thing. We take today's format for granted, with its handy lists of ingredients, precise measurements, and hold-my-hand instructions, but the earliest collections of recipes were mere guidelines, often quite vague, assuming that the reader was already well versed in the art of cookery.

Reading them is fun and puzzling, because of the changes in language and spelling in particular, and can conjure up romantic visions of kitchens past: stone floors polished by the shuffling of so many feet, pewter pots simmering away in large hearths, and freshly killed game hanging from a nail somewhere. I also love to read about the old-fashioned dishes they describe, how they were made and served, and how they traveled through the centuries to be handed down to the modern cook.

Blanc-manger is among these: it can be traced back to the fourteenth century, and its name means, quite simply, white food (*mengier* is Old French for food, or meal). The recipe evolved over time, alternating between the sweet and the savory, until it settled on its contemporary form, a smooth white dessert molded in ramekins. Its consistency is similar to the Italian *panna cotta*, slightly gelled yet creamy, but its distinctive taste comes from almond milk — milk in which crushed almonds have been steeped to deliver their flavor.

I make blanc-manger with a mix of almonds and hazelnuts — the flavor is bolder that way — and serve it with a basil coulis. In addition to the eye-catching color contrast, this topping, if served light-handedly, provides a surprising taste-bud experience: basil is seldom used in desserts, but its grassy flavor is an excellent complement to the nuttiness of the blanc-manger. Because basil coulis is somewhat better suited to the adventurous palate, I have also included a recipe for its raspberry sibling, which you can ladle on more generously. A simple sprinkle of fresh berries is a swell option, too.

1. In a food processor, chop the almonds and hazelnuts until they are reduced to small chunks, but not quite powdered. Reserve 2 tablespoons and combine the rest with the

milk in a medium saucepan. Bring to a simmer over medium heat, remove from heat, cover, and let stand for 10 minutes.

2. In the meantime, whisk together the cream, sugar, and agar-agar in a medium mixing bowl (if you use sheets of gelatin, don't add them yet; if you use granulated gelatin, add it now, and let the mixture stand for 5 minutes).

3. Set a fine-mesh sieve over the mixing bowl and pour the milk mixture through the sieve. Press the nuts with a wooden spoon to strain as much of the liquids as you can. Reserve the nuts for another use (see Note). Whisk the milk mixture to combine.

4. Rinse the saucepan and pour the milk mixture back into it. (If you use sheets of gelatin, add them to the pan now.) Cook over medium-low heat, stirring regularly with a wooden spoon, until the mixture just starts to simmer (if you use sheets of gelatin, make sure they are dissolved). Pour into the mixing bowl through the sieve and let cool for 5 minutes. Stir and pour into 6-ounce ramekins or glasses. Transfer cautiously to the fridge and chill until set, about an hour. This can be prepared up to a day ahead.

5. Remove from the fridge 5 minutes before serving. Top each ramekin with a spoonful of coulis (see recipes on page 204), sprinkle with the reserved nuts, and serve.

NOTE You can make cookies with the leftover nuts: whisk them with 1 egg, $^1/_4$ cup sugar, 2 tablespoons honey, $^1/_4$ cup flour, and 1 teaspoon lemon zest. Chill for an hour. Drop tablespoons of batter onto a greased baking sheet and bake at 400°F for 10 minutes, until golden but still a bit soft. Let cool and eat within a day or two.

*W*INE RÉMY PANNIER 2004 VOUVRAY (France, Loire, white) This demi-sec Vouvray is just slightly sweet, with a good acidity. It has the delicate fruitiness of pear, with flavors of honey and lime, and a lavender, herbal note.

1 cup whole blanched almonds

1 cup whole hazelnuts, with or without skin

1^1/2 cups milk

1 cup light cream

^{1}/3 cup sugar

1 teaspoon powdered agar-agar, a seaweed-based gelling agent that can be found in organic and natural foods stores (substitute 1^1/2 sheets gelatin, soaked in a bowl of cold water for 10 minutes and squeezed dry, or 1 teaspoon granulated gelatin)

Serves 4 (the recipe can also be used to make 6 small servings)
Chilling time: 1 hour

Blanc-Manger au Coulis de Basilic ou Framboise
Blancmange with Basil or Raspberry Coulis, page 200

Brioche aux Amandes, Poire & Chocolat
Almond, Pear, and Chocolate Brioche, page 204

Basil Coulis

1 cup (packed) fresh basil leaves

2 tablespoons confectioners' sugar

2 tablespoons extra virgin olive oil

*Makes about ¹/4 cups
(enough for 4 to 6 blancmange)*

Combine all the ingredients in a food processor. Process in short pulses until smooth. Taste and add a little more sugar if desired, but the coulis shouldn't be too sweet. Pour into an airtight container and chill for up to a day, or freeze.

Raspberry Coulis

1 cup fresh raspberries, about $^1/2$ pint, quickly rinsed and patted dry

2 tablespoons confectioners' sugar

*Makes about ¹/2 cups
(enough for 4 to 6 blancmange)*

Combine the raspberries, sugar, and 1 tablespoon water in a food processor. Process in short pulses until smooth. Taste and add a little more sugar if desired, but the coulis shouldn't be too sweet. You can strain the coulis through a medium-mesh sieve to remove the seeds, but this is optional (I never do). Pour into an airtight container and chill for up to a day, or freeze. This coulis is great on ice cream or yogurt cake (see page 178), or drizzled on a thick and generously buttered slice of fresh bread.

BRIOCHE AUX AMANDES, POIRE & CHOCOLAT

Almond, Pear, and Chocolate Brioche

On Saturday mornings, my father would take my sister and me to his favorite store for comic books and graphic novels in the Latin Quarter. The three of us would spend what felt like hours in that small shop, browsing through the new *bandes des-*

sinées releases, digging for undiscovered gems in the wooden boxes, and reading cross-legged in a corner.

After stepping out of the store with our purchases, we would walk to a nearby bakery-cum-café, where we would sit at the counter and start reading through the week's harvest, after a bit of negotiation as to who would read what first. My father would order an espresso, we girls a *diabolo menthe* (lemonade with mint syrup), and all three of us would indulge in a *croissant aux amandes*, a flaky croissant filled with almond cream, topped with sliced almonds and a snowfall of confectioners' sugar. This was pure buttery bliss, the elbows of the croissant having crisped up and caramelized in the oven while its heart remained tender and chewy.

The croissant aux amandes, which also exists in a *pain au chocolat* version, is yet another proof that necessity is the mother of brilliant invention: originally devised as a way to recycle day-old croissants, the resulting pastry is just as good as what it's meant to do away with, if not better. The following recipe applies the same idea to day-old slices of brioche. I will however admit that I sometimes buy a loaf and let it go stale on purpose to make these puffy golden treats, topped with almond cream, slices of pears, and a sprinkle of chocolate chips. Serve for dessert, as an afternoon snack, or for brunch.

FOR THE POACHED PEARS

2 tablespoons sugar

2 tablespoons light rum (optional)

2 ripe pears, about 1 pound (choose a variety that will retain its shape when poached, such as Bosc, Winter Nellis, or Anjou), quartered, cored, and peeled

FOR THE ALMOND CREAM

$1/2$ cup sugar

$3/4$ cup whole blanched almonds

$1/4$ teaspoon salt

8 tablespoons (1 stick) butter, at room temperature

2 large eggs

Eight $3/4$-inch-thick slices day-old brioche or challah bread, about 7 ounces total

$1/4$ cup good-quality bittersweet or semisweet chocolate chips (substitute $1^1/2$ ounces chocolate, chopped, or chilled and cut in shavings with a vegetable peeler)

Serves 4 to 8

1. **Poach the pears:** combine 1 cup water, the sugar, and the rum, if using, in a medium saucepan. Bring to a simmer over medium heat. Add the pears to the saucepan. Once the mixture starts to simmer again, cook for 4 minutes, until cooked through and slightly translucent. Remove from heat and let cool.

2. **Prepare the almond cream:** combine the sugar, almonds, and salt in a food processor and mix until finely ground. Add the butter and mix again until blended. Add the

eggs one by one and process until creamy. (You can prepare the pears and almond cream up to a day in advance. Transfer to separate airtight containers, leaving the pears in the syrup, and refrigerate.)

3. Preheat the oven to 350°F and line a baking sheet with parchment paper. Remove the pear pieces from the syrup with a slotted spoon and slice them thinly and horizontally, making sure they retain their shape.

4. Dip each side of the brioche slices lightly in the syrup. If the slices seem too fragile to be dipped without falling apart, use a pastry brush to coat. Arrange on the baking sheet. Spread 2 tablespoons almond cream on each slice, working carefully to avoid tearing. Use the blade of a knife to lift each pear quarter, press gently on the slices of pear to fan them out, and transfer onto each piece of brioche.

5. Bake for 15 minutes, until the almond cream is set and golden. Transfer to a rack and let cool for 5 minutes. Sprinkle with chocolate chips and serve slightly warm or at room temperature. (In the unlikely event that you have leftovers, they will keep for up to a day, wrapped in foil and refrigerated. Reheat for 5 minutes in a 350°F oven.)

VARIATIONS Instead of poached pears, top the brioche with raspberries, sliced strawberries, or quartered figs — no need to cook any of these fruits first.

WINE BONNY DOON 2004 MUSCAT VIN DE GLACIÈRE (USA, California, ice-style white) Sweet, but with a nice, balancing acidity, this dessert wine offers aromas of roasted pears, peaches, and honey. The palate is similarly fruity, accented by butterscotch and caramel flavors, and a distinctive honey-nut character.

COMPOTE D'ABRICOTS À LA LAVANDE

Lavender Apricot Compote

*O*n one of the shopping streets in Montmartre is a store that specializes in imported spices, aromatic herbs, and choice condiments. There is something supernatural about this shop, as it seems to carry every quirky seasoning ingredient I could possibly look for: all I have to do is rub the magic lamp, make a wish, and the shopkeeper will smile, nod, and point me to the appropriate shelf, basket, or barrel.

Even when I don't have anything specific in mind, I like to linger inside, study the labels, and buy whatever intrigues and appeals. And this is how I once acquired a small bag of dried lavender flowers. Once home, I transferred them into a glass jar so I could better admire the pastel buds. I wasn't entirely sure what to do with them and was quite content with the occasional refreshing whiff, until I was one day inspired to add a few specks to an apricot compote. This turned out to be a superb pairing, the scent of lavender vibrating against the apricots, teasing their acidulated flavor, and giving an air of low-key sophistication to this otherwise simple dessert.

1. Melt the butter in a large skillet over medium-low heat. Sprinkle with sugar and let it melt without stirring for 3 to 5 minutes, until blond and lightly caramelized. Add the salt and the apricots and stir to coat. Cover and cook until tender, about 8 minutes.

2. Remove the fruit from the skillet with a slotted spoon and set aside in a large bowl, leaving as much of the cooking juices as you can in the skillet. Sprinkle the lavender over the juices, turn the heat to medium-high, and cook uncovered until thick and syrupy, 4 to 5 minutes, stirring regularly. (I leave the lavender buds in the compote, but if you think you might be bothered

2 tablespoons unsalted butter

¹/₄ cup sugar

A pinch of fine sea salt

2 pounds fresh ripe apricots, halved and pitted

2 teaspoons dried unsprayed edible lavender flowers (see page 208)

Serves 4 to 6

by them, strain the reduced juices through a fine-mesh sieve into a bowl. Discard the lavender, and return the juices to the skillet.)

3. Return the apricots to the skillet and stir delicately to coat. Let cool until slightly warm or at room temperature. Serve with ladyfingers or thin butter cookies.

VARIATIONS This compote can also be made with peaches or plums.

*W*INE MARCARINI 2004 MOSCATO D'ASTI (Italy, Piedmont, sparkling white) Light on the palate and low in alcohol, this sweet bubbly wine manages to avoid heaviness thanks to its light spritzy fizz. The aromas are lightly floral to touch on the lavender, with white and yellow peach notes that echo the apricot.

CRÈME DE RICOTTA À LA MANGUE, CROUSTILLANT DE MACADAMIA

Creamy Mango Ricotta with Macadamia Crunch

I have a strange passion for serving dishes, be they sweet or savory, in transparent glasses. It has become quite popular in restaurants (on French menus the magic word is *verrine*), but I don't see it as yet another fad: showcasing colors and textures in neat, attractive layers does bring an additional dimension to the eating experience.

This dessert is a tasty illustration: as the diner digs in, the spoon first meets crunchy clusters of caramelized oats and macadamia nuts. It then proceeds across a smooth layer of lightly sweetened ricotta, before it finally reaches the juicy mango

Serving glasses

Glasses are best used to serve dishes that are cold, at room temperature, or just slightly warm. Reserve this treatment for preparations that do have different colors and textures to display, most often first courses and desserts. Arrange the ingredients in contrasting layers, and take it slow to avoid smudging the sides of the glass. This type of dish can usually be prepared ahead of time, but if one of the components is crisp or crunchy, add it to the top and at the last minute so it won't turn soggy.

Compote d'Abricots à la Lavande
Lavender Apricot Compote, page 207

Crème de Ricotta à la Mangue, Croustillant de Macadamia
Creamy Mango Ricotta with Macadamia Crunch, page 208

1 tablespoon butter

3 tablespoons maple syrup

$^1/_2$ cup old-fashioned rolled oats (or a mix of several rolled grains)

$^1/_4$ teaspoon fine sea salt

$^1/_3$ cup macadamia nuts, roughly chopped

$^1/_2$ teaspoon (lightly packed) freshly grated lime zest, from an organic lime

$1^1/_4$ cups ricotta cheese, about 11 ounces, preferably artisanal

3 tablespoons confectioners' sugar

$^1/_3$ cup light cream

2 cups diced mango flesh, from about $1^1/_2$ large ripe mangoes

2 teaspoons freshly squeezed lime juice

Serves 4 to 6

chunks at the bottom. And as the spoon makes its way back up to the surface, it naturally gathers a cross section of the different elements, adding up to the perfect bite.

1. Preheat the oven to 350°F and line a baking sheet with parchment paper. Combine the butter and maple syrup in a small saucepan and set over medium heat until the butter is just melted. Remove from heat.

2. Combine the oats, salt, nuts, and zest in a medium mixing bowl. Pour in the butter mixture and stir to combine. Spread over the baking sheet and bake for 12 minutes, until golden, stirring the mixture once or twice as it bakes. Remove from the oven and let cool. (This can be prepared a few days ahead and kept in an airtight container. It is also great as a snack or breakfast treat, sprinkled over yogurt.)

3. Clean the mixing bowl you used to prepare the topping and use it to combine the ricotta and sugar. Using a manual or an electric whisk, beat the mixture until smooth. Add the cream and whisk again until thoroughly combined.

4. In a medium bowl, gently toss the diced mango with the lime juice. Divide the mango among glasses and top with the ricotta mixture. This can be prepared up to 4 hours ahead: cover and refrigerate until 10 minutes before serving.

5. Just before serving, sprinkle each glass with 2 tablespoons topping. Pour the rest of the topping in a small bowl and set it on the table so crunch enthusiasts can help themselves to more.

*W*INE MACARI VINEYARDS 2003 BLOCK E (USA, New York, ice-style white) The nose of this wine is nutty, floral, and fruity all at once. The palate is ripe and rich, with notes of honey, crisp pear, and tropical fruit — mango in particular. Not cloying in the least, it offers a lively acidity and a long, elegant finish.

CRÊPES

$\mathscr{A}$side from a trip to the Alps every summer, the other traditional vacation for my family was to spend a week in Brittany in the spring. Our destination of choice was Carnac, a small town on the southern coast, famous for its stunning menhir alignments.

The weather was always a bit of a gamble, as this time of year had equal chances of being brightly sunny or grimly overcast and thunderous, but I would be hard-pressed to say the kind of weather I preferred. I loved riding my bike up and down the shoreline until I had sunburn on the back of my hands, or building lofty sandcastles that we fought to protect against the rising tide. But I also enjoyed watching sea storms from the safety of the shore, jumping in delighted fear as the waves came crashing against the pier, and coming home, red-cheeked and drippy-nosed, hardly seeing a thing through my soaking wet, salt-crusted glasses.

I also have many edible memories from those vacations. In Carnac we knew every bakery, and which one sold the best *kouign-amann* (a caramelized flaked pastry that calls for indecent amounts of butter); every ice-cream parlor, and which one had the tastiest waffle cones and most interesting flavors; every *crêperie*, and which one served the best crêpes.

CRÊPE FILLINGS *Popular fillings include the classic and unsurpassable combo of salted butter and sugar; jam, especially stone fruit and berry; sugar and lemon juice; Nutella or melted chocolate, to which you can add sliced bananas; chestnut cream; caramel sauce; maple syrup or honey; and stewed fruit, especially apples. Whipped cream and ice cream are dandy additions, too.* ❀

For Brittany is the homeland of crêpes, and that's what we had for dinner every single night, to the sparkly-eyed joy of my sister and myself: dining out was an exceptional treat for us, and eating crêpes on a daily basis was very much our idea of heaven.

In Brittany, savory crêpes are made with buckwheat flour, and depending on the area they are called *galettes* or *crêpes de sarrasin*. These are difficult to get right at home: for impeccably thin, crackly-edged crêpes, you need excellent flour, an expert hand,

and a large crêpe maker to ensure even heat distribution. Sweet crêpes, on the other hand, call for regular wheat flour and couldn't be simpler to make — the one easier option being to run downstairs and buy one from the little stand across the street with the brooding old man and the faded beach umbrella.

Crêpes are the traditional food with which French families celebrate *La Chandeleur* (Candlemas) on February 2, a holiday that bids farewell to winter and welcomes the first shimmers of spring. This tradition comes with various superstitious little tricks to bring happiness and prosperity upon the household: one of them involves holding a coin in your left hand — a gold coin works best, but a euro will do — as you flip the crêpe in the pan with your right hand. If all goes smoothly and you haven't dropped the crêpe, or the coin, or hit the ceiling with the crêpe, chances are you're lying. But if you're not, that is a very good omen.

However, crêpes can be enjoyed in any season: kids adore them, and they are a fun interactive dessert for a small gathering of friends. As the crêpes are made and served, each diner garnishes his with the filling of his choice, rolls it into a log or folds it in four, and eats it, preferably with his fingers. Crêpes are just as good at room temperature — spread them lightly with jam or sugar, fold them in four, and wrap in foil for a picnic.

1^2/3 cups all-purpose flour

^{1}/4 teaspoon fine sea salt

^{1}/4 cup sugar

2 teaspoons pure vanilla extract

3 large eggs, lightly beaten

1 cup milk

2 tablespoons light rum (optional)

2 tablespoons unsalted butter

Vegetable oil for the skillet

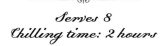

Serves 8
Chilling time: 2 hours

1. Pour the flour in a large mixing bowl and form a well in the center. Add the salt, sugar, vanilla, and eggs to the well. Whisk gently in the center so the eggs will blend with part — not all — of the flour. Pour in the milk and 1 cup filtered or spring water slowly, whisking as you pour. Keep whisking until all the flour is incorporated; the batter will be thin. Add the rum, if using, and whisk again. Cover the bowl with plastic wrap and refrigerate for 2 hours, or preferably overnight.

2. Melt the butter in a small saucepan. Remove the batter from the refrigerator, whisk again for a few seconds, and pour through a fine-mesh sieve into another bowl: this will remove any lumps of flour from the batter. Whisk in the melted butter.

3. Set a thick-bottomed, low-rimmed skillet over high heat. Wait until it is very hot, enough to make a drop of water sizzle. Spray the pan with good-quality vegetable oil, or dip a folded paper towel in a ramekin that contains a little vegetable oil and wipe it over the pan to grease it lightly (watch your fingers).

4. Ladle a little batter in the pan, just enough to thinly cover the pan, and swish the pan around in a slow circular motion so the batter forms a round disk. Cook for 40 seconds, or until the edges start to turn golden and pull slightly away from the sides. Run the tip of a hard spatula around the crêpe to loosen, peek underneath, and flip the crêpe when you see that it is nice and golden. Cook for 20 more seconds on the other side, or until golden as well, and slip out of the pan onto a plate. (Note that the first crêpe of the batch is usually a dud.) Grease the skillet again every two or three crêpes.

5. Serve the crêpes from the skillet as you make them, or pile them on a heatproof plate set over a saucepan of simmering water, covering the crêpes with foil until ready to serve. The batter and crêpes will keep for 2 to 3 days in the fridge, tightly covered.

VARIATIONS Instead of rum and vanilla, flavor the batter with Grand Marnier and orange zest.

Even though it isn't quite traditional, this recipe can be adapted for savory fillings: omit the sugar, vanilla, and rum, and up the amount of salt to ½ teaspoon. Fill the crêpes with ham, grated Gruyère, and an egg, sunny side up (a classic called *la complète*); leeks and goat cheese; fresh tomatoes and Comté; smoked salmon and crème fraîche.

𝒟RINKS Crêpes are traditionally paired with hard cider from Brittany or with a type of fermented milk called *lait ribot:* kefir is a good substitute.

Mignardises

SWEET BITES

Billes de Noisettes au Chocolat
CHOCOLATE-DIPPED HAZELNUT MARBLES

Navettes à la Fleur d'Oranger
ORANGE FLOWER SHUTTLE COOKIES

Sablés au Citron
LEMON BUTTER COOKIES

Mini-Financiers au Miel
HONEY ALMOND BITES

Biscuits Très Chocolat
VERY CHOCOLATE COOKIES

BILLES DE NOISETTES AU CHOCOLAT

Chocolate-Dipped Hazelnut Marbles

Mignardises (meen-yard-eez) are the sweet bites that you get with coffee after a meal at a fancy restaurant. The word stems from *mignard*, which means pretty, delicate, and graceful — such a promising description. A mignardise tray will typically feature tiny cookies, miniature versions of pastries (*canelés* and *financiers* in particular), nougat, fruit pastes, or filled chocolates. I find them quite irresistible, and I confess that I often order coffee not so much for the drink itself as for the dainty nibbles that I hope will appear in its wake.

Mignardises make for excellent kitchen projects in that they require a bit of craftiness, an eye for detail, and a reasonable talent for the shaping and handling of small-size objects. This means they can be a bit time-consuming, but as with any other crafty activity, the idea is to enjoy the process — a teammate is welcome, too. And once you have your little army of confections neatly lined up on the counter, the gratification is immense. At that point, you may summon the other members of the household so they can voice their admiration and filch a few of your creations when you're not looking.

I make mignardises to serve at the end of a dinner party, as is their intended purpose, or wrap them up and give them away. I might note here that homemade food gifts aren't as common in France as they are in America: a box of chocolate or candy is a widespread hostess gift, but most of the time it will be bought from a pastry shop. In my experience, however, the French are just as appreciative of that personal touch — perhaps even more so, since they're not used to receiving a pretty beribboned package with a hand-inscribed tag and a dozen freshly made confections inside.

I also like to serve mignardises when I have friends over for an afternoon cup of tea. Beyond the sophistication that they bring to the occasion, they are also less imposing on my guests' appetite: they can eat however much or little they want without feeling pressured to eat a whole slice of cake, when perhaps they've feasted like Gargantua all week long, and all they wish for is a tisane and a celery stalk.

The following mignardises-on-a-stick are made of a marzipan-like hazelnut paste that is shaped into marbles and dipped in bittersweet chocolate. Keep the marbles small for an optimal chocolate-to-hazelnut ratio and serve on a tiny plate with coffee.

1. Combine the hazelnuts, sugar, and salt in a food processor and pulse until finely ground. Transfer to a medium mixing bowl and form a well in the center. In a small bowl, combine the honey with 1 tablespoon hot water and stir to dissolve. Pour into the center of the hazelnut mixture and stir with a fork to blend.

1 cup shelled hazelnuts, toasted and husked (see page 6)

^{3}/4 cup confectioners' sugar

A pinch of fine sea salt

2 teaspoons honey (grease your measuring spoon with a little vegetable oil)

3 ounces good-quality bittersweet chocolate

Makes about 25 marbles
Resting/chilling time:
1 hour for the hazelnut
paste, 2 hours for the
finished marbles

2. Knead the hazelnut paste for a minute or two, until it comes together and you are able to shape it into a ball. (It will be a little sticky, but it will dry as it chills.) Wrap in plastic and refrigerate for at least an hour, and up to a day.

3. Remove the hazelnut paste from the fridge. Scoop out rounded teaspoons and shape them into small balls, about ^{3}/4 inch in diameter, with the tips of your fingers. Line them up on a plate and plant a wooden toothpick vertically in the center of each. Cover loosely with plastic wrap and place the plate in the fridge.

4. Line a baking sheet with parchment paper. Melt the chocolate in a double boiler or in a heatproof bowl set over a pan of simmering water, stirring from time to time.

5. Dip each of the marbles in turn in the chocolate, holding it by the toothpick and swirling it around gently to coat. Leave the very top uncoated, so the hazelnut paste shows. Lift from the chocolate, let the excess chocolate drip down for a few seconds, and set on the parchment paper, toothpick pointing skyward. Let rest somewhere cool (but not the refrigerator) for 2 hours, until the chocolate coating is dry. The marbles will keep for up to 4 days at room temperature in an airtight container.

VARIATIONS The marbles can be made with other nuts, such as almonds or pecans.

Billes de Noisettes au Chocolat
Chocolate-Dipped Hazelnut Marbles, page 218

Navettes à la Fleur d'Oranger
Orange Flower Shuttle Cookies, page 222

NAVETTES À LA FLEUR D'ORANGER

Orange Flower Shuttle Cookies

Navettes are a specialty from Provence, in the southeast of France. These cookies get their name from their oval shuttle shape, in Christian honor of the boat that brought the *Saintes Maries* to the Provençal coast two thousand years ago, three women who were fleeing Palestine after the crucifixion of Jesus, and stayed on to evangelize the area.

Maxence and I sampled our first navettes on a completely agnostic weekend trip to Marseille one summer, as we were strolling around the historic city center on a blazing hot afternoon. In the maze of narrow cobbled streets, a bakery happened upon our path, just as we were starting to feel like a snack — or maybe my built-in radar had been steering us all along, I'm not quite sure.

The antithesis of the bright and cheerful bakeries I am used to, this one was full of shadows and eerily quiet, giving off the distinct impression that everyone inside was taking a nap, like any sensible Marseillais would do at this time of day and in this heat. Still, the door was unlocked, so we called out a tentative *"Bonjour?"* After a few minutes of near-perfect silence — a clock ticking somewhere, a cough, the ruffle of sheets — a lady emerged from the back in slipper-clad, trailing footsteps. She walked sleepily to the register, sold us a dozen of her golden navettes, and disappeared without a word. We walked out, blinking in the sudden sunlight, and resumed our stroll, our knuckles colliding in the paper bag.

Navettes are dry and crunchy cookies that reveal a tender and crumbly heart. Not too sweet and not too rich, they are friendly companions to a cup of tea or coffee — dunking is allowed, and even encouraged. Depending on where you buy your navettes, their shape, texture, and taste will vary, but my preference goes to this version, subtly flavored with orange flower water.

1. Combine the butter and sugar in a food processor and process until fluffy. Add the egg and orange flower water and mix until blended. Add the flour and salt and mix

until smooth. Turn out the dough on a lightly floured surface and knead gently until it forms a ball. Add a touch more flour if the dough is too moist, or a little ice-cold water, a teaspoon at a time, if it is too dry. Divide the dough into two slightly flattened balls, wrap each half in plastic, and refrigerate for an hour, or up to a day.

2. Preheat the oven to 350°F and line a baking sheet with parchment paper.

3. Remove one ball of dough from the refrigerator and divide it into eight equal pieces. Roll each piece with the palm of your hand on your work surface until it forms a log, about 3 inches in length. Cut the log in two with a knife so you have two 1^{1}/2-inch logs, and set aside. Repeat with the other pieces until you have sixteen small logs.

4 tablespoons (^{1}/2 stick) unsalted butter, at room temperature

^{1}/2 cup sugar

1 large egg, lightly beaten

3 tablespoons orange flower water (substitute 3 tablespoons fresh water plus 1 tablespoon grated orange zest, finely chopped, from an organic orange)

2 cups all-purpose flour

^{1}/4 teaspoon fine sea salt

1 large egg yolk, lightly beaten with 1 tablespoon fresh water

Makes 32 cookies
Chilling time: 1 hour

4. Pinch the ends of each log and flatten the top slightly, to form a boat shape. With the tip of a round-ended knife, carve a deep slit lengthwise down the center, not quite reaching the other side or the ends. Arrange the cookies on the baking sheet and repeat with the second half of the dough.

5. Brush with the egg yolk mixture. Bake for 15 minutes, until golden and slightly browned at the tips. Transfer to a rack to cool completely and serve with coffee or tea. The navettes will keep for a couple of weeks at room temperature in an airtight container. They will harden after the first few days, but you can revive their initial texture by reheating them for 3 to 4 minutes at 350°F — in Provence, they claim that a bit of their sunshine does the trick. The dough can also be frozen for up to a month.

VARIATIONS For a more pronounced orange flavor, up the amount of orange flower water by a tablespoon, or use both orange zest and orange flower water. You can also omit the orange flavoring and add finely ground hazelnuts, finely chopped raisins, or freshly ground pink peppercorns to the dough.

SABLÉS AU CITRON

Lemon Butter Cookies

When my older sister left for Germany on a two-year study abroad program, I was devastated. Céline was my confidante, my accomplice, we thought the same things and finished each other's sentences, we teamed up to get our parents to let us do stuff, we fought over capital things such as who should clear the table, she let me borrow her beige jacket . . . What was I going to do without her?

I allowed myself a few good cries, sitting on the floor of her bedroom (much larger than mine, I might add) and thinking how much I missed her, until I got used to her absence and it felt a bit less painful. Of course, it wasn't so much the distance that made me cry — Frankfurt isn't exactly on another planet — but rather that her departure rang like the official end of our childhood. She was flying off the nest on her brand-new wings, my turn would come soon, and part of me wished I could stop time from moving so fast.

I remember the parting gift I gave her: it was a set of heart-shaped cookie cutters, held together by a metal ring. In the box I had included our mother's recipe for lemon butter cookies, which I'd written up as a story about pixies with pointy hats baking up a storm in their hollow tree-trunk houses. These were the cookies we liked to make on Sunday afternoons, taking turns cutting out flowers and stars, popping stray strips of dough into our mouths, and wiping the bowl of glaze clean with our fingers.

The recipe is still safely inscribed in the spiral recipe book I started around that time, and I bake up a batch of these sablés every time I want something buttery and delicate to have with tea, when I crave their fresh citrus flavor and the way they crunch between your teeth, then melt upon your tongue.

During the holiday season I use this recipe to make cut-out cookies, but for a speedier preparation I switch to the simple slice-and-bake method. When I was a child we always flavored them with lemon, but orange and lime are pleasing variations.

1. Grate the lemon to yield a tablespoon of finely chopped lemon zest. Reserve the lemon for the glaze.

2. In a large mixing bowl, combine the flour, granulated sugar, salt, and lemon zest. Add the butter and rub it into the dry ingredients with the tips of your fingers or use a wire pastry blender. Add the egg yolk, stir with a fork until blended, and knead the dough until it comes together and forms a ball. If the dough is too dry, add a little ice-cold water, a teaspoon at a time, and knead again. If it is too sticky, add 1 tablespoon flour.

3. Divide the dough in two and roll each half into a log, about 1 inch in diameter. Wrap each log in plastic and put in the freezer for 30 minutes.

4. Preheat the oven to 350°F and line a baking sheet with parchment paper. Remove one log of dough from the freezer, unwrap, and slice in $1/4$-inch rounds with a sharp serrated knife, rotating the log by a quarter of a turn after each slice so it keeps a rounded shape. Transfer onto the baking sheet, leaving a $1/2$-inch margin between them. Repeat with the second log.

5. Bake for 12 minutes, until lightly golden at the edges. Transfer to a rack and let cool completely before glazing, about an hour.

6. Squeeze the lemon to get 3 tablespoons lemon juice. Put the confectioners' sugar in a bowl, add the lemon juice, and whisk until smooth and syrupy. Use a pastry brush or the back of a teaspoon to glaze the cookies. Let stand until the glaze is set, about an hour. The cookies will keep for up to a week at room temperature in an airtight container. The dough can also be frozen for up to a month.

1 organic lemon

1 cup plus 2 tablespoons all-purpose flour

$1/3$ cup granulated sugar

1 teaspoon fleur de sel or kosher salt

7 tablespoons ($3^{1}/2$ ounces) chilled unsalted butter, diced

1 large egg yolk

1 cup confectioners' sugar

Makes about 40 small cookies
Chilling time: 30 minutes for the dough, 1 hour for cooling, 1 hour for the glaze to set

Sablés au Citron
Lemon Butter Cookies, page 224

Mini-Financiers au Miel
Honey Almond Bites, page 228

MINI-FINANCIERS AU MIEL

Honey Almond Bites

𝒯he classic financier is a small rectangular almond cake that bears an uncanny resemblance to a gold ingot, hence the name. Consider its frail, crisp edges, its tender heart made slightly nubby by the presence of ground almonds, and its pervasive flavor of nutty butter: need I further explain the popularity of this superlative, and disarmingly easy-to-make confection?

Because financiers are rather rich (unless they make unfortunate investments and go bankrupt), I like to bake them into miniature bites, to be enjoyed with coffee after a meal or a cup of tea in the afternoon. The traditional recipe calls for sugar, but using honey gives them a haunting depth of flavor: I have a weakness for the sappy aromas of chestnut honey or the mildness of spring honey, but you can use any kind of quality honey, preferably artisanal.

1 cup whole blanched almonds

$^1/_3$ cup sugar

3 tablespoons all-purpose flour

$^1/_4$ teaspoon fine sea salt

6 tablespoons unsalted butter, plus extra for greasing molds

$^1/_3$ cup good-quality honey (grease your measuring cup with a little vegetable oil)

2 large eggs or 4 large egg whites

Makes 20 to 60 pieces, depending on the size of your molds
Chilling time: 1 hour

1. In a food processor, mix the almonds and sugar until finely ground. Combine with the flour and salt in a medium mixing bowl and set aside.

2. Melt the butter in a small saucepan over medium-low heat. When it starts to simmer, cook for 2 minutes, until it becomes golden brown and starts to smell nutty (this is called *beurre noisette*). Add the honey and stir to melt.

3. Pour the butter mixture into the dry ingredients and whisk until combined. Add the eggs one by one, whisking well after each addition. Pour the batter into a 1-gallon food storage bag (preferably the twist-tie kind), squeeze out all the air, and close tightly with a knot (or zip closed). This is the homemade version of a pastry bag (which you can use if you have one, of course), and it makes the filling of the molds much neater than using a spoon. Chill for an hour.

4. Preheat the oven to 350°F and grease a tray of micro-muffin (or mini-muffin) molds with butter. (This is unnecessary if they're nonstick, silicone, or otherwise blessed with magic powers.)

5. Remove the bag from the fridge and snip the very tip of one corner with scissors to create a $1/4$-inch opening. Press on the bag to pipe the batter into the prepared molds, filling them almost to the rim.

6. Bake for 12 to 16 minutes, depending on the size of your molds, until golden and set. Let stand for a few minutes, unmold, and transfer to a rack to cool completely. (The financiers will keep for 4 days at room temperature in an airtight container. They can also be frozen for up to a month.)

VARIATIONS To make classic financiers, omit the honey and up the amount of sugar to $1/2$ cup plus 2 tablespoons. You can also use half almonds and half hazelnuts, plop a raspberry into each mold before baking, or add 1 tablespoon finely grated citrus zest to the dry ingredients.

BISCUITS TRÈS CHOCOLAT

Very Chocolate Cookies

*I*f chocolate shops were chocolate chips, Paris would be one super-loaded cookie. The city is blessed with dozens of excellent chocolatiers, fine artisans who pride themselves on selecting the best chocolate, or even processing their own cacao beans.

Whenever I walk by one of these shops, my feet propel me inside of their own accord. I take deep breaths to stock up on the rich scents, study the selection carefully,

Cacao nibs Roasted cacao nibs are tiny bits of roasted cocoa beans, not sweetened or processed any further. They are crunchy and have a quintessential chocolate flavor. You can find them at gourmet and specialty foods stores: they are not cheap, but a little goes a long way, and they are very versatile. Add them to sweet preparations (jams, muffins, cakes, scones, crumble or streusel toppings) or savory ones (spice rubs, poultry stuffing, sauces, or pasta — see page 102). Chocolate-coated cacao nibs will work fine in this recipe, and if you can't find them at all, substitute toasted and finely chopped nuts, such as hazelnuts, walnuts, or pecans.

ask the salesperson for advice, and walk away with the chocolate bar of my choice, elegantly wrapped and safely tucked at the bottom of my purse — were I to be the victim of pickpockets, I'd rather lose my wallet.

As a result, I always have one or two or six half-eaten bars in my secret chocolate stash (why I keep it a secret is beyond me, since Maxence doesn't even like the bittersweet stuff I favor), from which I break off little chunks to savor with my post-lunch coffee shot.

As far as espresso companions go, it's hard to beat a simple square of ebony chocolate, but these tiny turbocharged cookies follow very closely. Crisp and crumbly, they get their intense chocolate flavor from four different sources: the velvet of melted chocolate, the smooth bite of chocolate chunks, the strength of cocoa powder, and the raw crunch of cacao nibs.

1. In a medium mixing bowl, sift together the flours, cocoa powder, and baking soda. Set aside.

2. Melt half of the chocolate ($2^{1}/2$ ounces) in a double boiler or in a heatproof bowl set over a pan of simmering water, stirring from time to time to dissolve. Set aside. Chop the remaining $2^{1}/2$ ounces chocolate into chip-size bits, combine with the cacao nibs, and set aside.

3. Put the butter in a food processor and process until creamy (you can also do this in a medium mixing bowl with a sturdy spatula). Add the sugar, salt, and vanilla, and mix until combined. Add the melted chocolate and mix again.

4. Add the reserved flour mixture and mix until just combined. Transfer the dough into the bowl you used for the flour mix: the next step needs to be done by hand. Fold the chopped chocolate and cacao nibs into the dough, working with a wooden spoon and/or your hands. The dough will be quite thick; don't overmix it.

$^{1}/2$ cup all-purpose flour

$^{1}/2$ cup whole wheat flour

$^{1}/4$ cup unsweetened Dutch-process cocoa powder

$^{1}/2$ teaspoon baking soda

5 ounces good-quality bittersweet chocolate

$^{1}/4$ cup roasted cacao nibs (see page 230)

$^{1}/2$ cup (1 stick) plus 1 tablespoon unsalted butter, at room temperature

$^{1}/2$ cup (packed) light brown sugar

$^{1}/2$ teaspoon fleur de sel or kosher salt (or $^{1}/4$ teaspoon fine sea salt)

1 teaspoon pure vanilla extract

Makes about 4 dozen bite-size cookies
Chilling time: 20 minutes

5. Cover the dough with plastic wrap and chill for 20 minutes. (You can chill it for up to a day — the dough will be a bit harder, but it will soften as you work with it. You can also wrap it tightly and freeze for up to a month.)

6. Preheat the oven to 350°F and line a baking sheet with parchment paper. Remove the dough from the fridge. Carve out rounded teaspoons of dough, shape them into slightly flattened balls with the tips of your fingers, and place them on the prepared baking sheet, separating them by $\frac{1}{2}$ inch. Bake for 10 to 12 minutes, until the tops are just set: the cookies will still be a little soft, but they will harden as they cool. Transfer the sheet of parchment paper cautiously to a rack and let cool completely. The cookies will keep for 4 days in an airtight container at room temperature, or they can be frozen for up to a month.

VARIATION Add $\frac{1}{2}$ to 1 teaspoon of ground *piment d'Espelette* (or any moderately hot ground chile powder) to the flour mixture: the heat of chile is a remarkable match to the warmth of the chocolate.

Biscuits Très Chocolat
Very Chocolate Cookies

Want More?

Log on to the *Chocolate & Zucchini* Web site (ChocolateandZucchini.com) for regular updates, more recipes, metric conversions, and forum discussions — a special section has been created in the forums for your questions and comments about this book. You can also e-mail the author at clotilde@clotilde.net.

INDEX